UFOs ABOVE PENNSYLVANIA

Gerard J. Medvec and Mark Sarro

Illustrations by Joyce Bensinger

4880 Lower Valley Road • Atglen, PA 19310

Schiffer Books are available at special discounts for bulk purchases for sales promotions or premiums. Special editions, including personalized covers, corporate imprints, and excerpts can be created in large quantities for special needs. For more information contact the publisher.

Published by Schiffer Publishing, Ltd.
4880 Lower Valley Road
Atglen, PA 19310
Phone: (610) 593-1777; Fax: (610) 593-2002
E-mail: Info@schifferbooks.com.

For the largest selection of fine reference books on this and related subjects,
please visit our website at
www.schifferbooks.com.
You may also write for a free catalog.

This book may be purchased from the publisher.
Please try your bookstore first.

We are always looking for people to write books on new and related subjects.
If you have an idea for a book, please contact us at
proposals@schifferbooks.com.

In Europe, Schiffer books are distributed by
Bushwood Books
6 Marksbury Ave.
Kew Gardens
Surrey TW9 4JF England
Phone: 44 (0) 20 8392 8585; Fax: 44 (0) 20 8392 9876
E-mail: info@bushwoodbooks.co.uk
Website: www.bushwoodbooks.co.uk

Other Schiffer Books by the Authors:

Ghosts of West Chester, Pennsylvania
ISBN: 978-0-7643-2996-8 $14.99

Haunted Gettysburg
ISBN: 978-0-7643-3310-1 $19.99

Ghosts of Delaware
ISBN: 978-0-7643-4139-7 $16.99

Registered Trademarks:
SPAM® is a registered trademark of Hormel Foods Corporation. ROAD RUNNER(R) is a registered trademark of Warner Bros. Inc. Jeep® and Neon® are registered trademarks of Chrysler, LLC. Jurassic Park® is a registered trademark of Universal Studios/Amblin Entertainment. STAR WARS® is a registered trademark of LucasArts Entertainment Company. Taurus® is a registered trademark of Ford Motor Company. Superman® and Wonder Woman® are registered trademarks of DC Comics. Dodge Neon® is a registered trademark of Chrysler, LLC. All-Star Converse® is a registered trademark of Converse, Inc. Sheriff Woody© and Buzz Lightyear© of Star Command:© Disney Enterprises, Inc. and Pixar Animation Studios. Adidas® is a registered trademark of Adidas, AG.
Cover image: Alien© Li-Bro. www.bigstockphoto.com

Designed by Mark David Bowyer
Type set in Century Gothic / Book Antiqua

ISBN: 978-0-7643-4292-9
Printed in the United States of America

Dedications

From Gerard J. Medvec

This book is for my beautiful wife, Joyce, my best friend.
Also for my wonderful daughters, Sabrina and Marissa,
and my good sons, Sagan and Landru.

It is also for the great state of independence—Pennsylvania.

From Mark Sarro

I dedicate this book to the planet Nibiru.

Acknowledgments

From Gerard J. Medvec

Thanks to Karen, the research associate at the International UFO Museum and Research Center in Roswell, New Mexico for her kind and quick help with information on sightings in Pennsylvania. Thanks to our editor, Dinah Roseberry, for straight-forward, no-nonsense help with a smile and a clear answer to all my inquiries. Thanks to Jo Ellen Frymaire, my dear friend, for pinching my memory back to alertness. Kudos to the geniuses who invented the Brainyquotes.com website. It is a full, fast, and fun site to use. Gratefulness to my dear wife, Joyce, for her artwork throughout the book, and her marksman-like, frontline editing of every written word. Thanks to my co-author and step-son, Mark, for all his efforts. Of course, if it was not for all the brave Pennsylvania UFO witnesses who shared their intimate stories, there would be nothing to read right now.

From Mark Sarro

I want to thank my friends and family for their continued support as I continue the journey to search for the answers to things that lie beyond us.

Contents

Epigraph

Truth does not become error because nobody sees it.

~Mohandas K. Gandhi
The Mahatma, political and
ideological leader of India

INTRODUCTION

Thank you for picking up this book. For the month of February 2012, MUFON (Mutual UFO Network) noted that they received 535 UFO reports in the United States alone. After California and Texas, the top two most populated states and two largest states in the lower forty-eight, the third highest rate of sightings, was in Pennsylvania. The Keystone State is only thirty-third in size and sixth in population, giving it a disproportionate amount of alien activity.

Stories of the paranormal are always difficult to relate. The languages of humans are just that: so primitive that they do not include words that adequately describe our perceptions of altered reality, especially when that reality relates to objects from, or actions of, other worldly beings. This includes the activities of multi-dimensional creatures and ethereal visitors from the afterlife. Add to this that many people simply keep their personal paranormal stories locked behind the door of a rigid social structure, because they have been rebuked or made fun of by family and peers, and you begin to feel the difficulty in getting these tales into print.

For the unwitting individual who glimpses a ball of light soaring above their house, or who has lost three hours of their life after an abduction, the need to tell their saga is paramount. They've experienced the bigger Universe, perhaps the entire Universe, and their outlook on their tiny life on this little planet has been upgraded forever.

Through the ensuing chapters, we wrestle with the English language, attempting to force it into revealing accurate and entertaining UFO experiences of our own—and others. You will decide who wins the match.

There are a lot of UFO books out there relating to many aspects of the same out-of-this-world phenomena. Often, the books are trying to convince you that it is all real. *UFOs Above Pennsylvania* is not about changing people's minds. It makes the assumption, based on the true personal experiences of both its authors, that alien existence and visitations to our planet on a regular basis *is reality*. Based on our observations of alien devices around the country, some of which you will read about, it seems likely that our nation alone is visited by tens of thousands of alien probes and devices every night. After reading the book, see if you agree.

Authors' Note on Geography

Despite this book being set in Pennsylvania, all the stories and blurbs printed here apply equally to all people around the world. It makes no difference if you are from Philadelphia on the Delaware River or from Filadelfeia, a suburb of Athens, Greece; no difference if you are from Bethlehem, Pennsylvania or Bethlehem, Israel; no difference if you are from the city of Indiana just east of Pittsburgh, or from the great state of Indiana. Tales similar, and in many cases nearly identical, to what you read here are happening all over the planet. It is now estimated on the web that around 100,000,000 people worldwide have reported experiencing some type of UFO event. My own estimate is that 2.5 *billion* folks have seen *something*.

If you reside in a state neighboring Pennsylvania, you may want a copy of this book to keep in your glove box, since most of the events we've written about are within an easy half-hour to two-hour ride from bordering towns in New York, New Jersey, Delaware, Maryland, Virginia, West Virginia, and Ohio. Even you Canadian folk can boat across Lake Erie and hang out at "alien central." Many of the full-length stories can be tracked down to actual locations so that a replication of an "experience" is theoretically possible. In at least one location, French Creek State Park in Chester and Berks Counties in Eastern Pennsylvania, it is not only possible to duplicate what I saw there on three separate occasions, it is almost guaranteed. If you camp out in Loop C for at least two or three nights, make sure you have your aluminum hat, a great camera, and a steel mill's-worth of nerve. You will most likely see some "thing."

The book is divided into three sections: Western, Central, and Eastern Pennsylvania, so that it is easy for locals to jump ahead to read about their neighborhood abnormalities. I am originally an eastern Pennsylvania kind of guy, being born in Southwest Philadelphia and having grown up in Yeadon, Delaware County. Most of my personal encounters with alien devices and other "things" have occurred in the southeastern part of the state.

Using the short story format to relay these tales was our idea. All the full-length works have been embellished with simple, believable minor details to make the reading fun. However, the UFO facts, be they the authors' or other storytellers', *are untainted and remain in the experiencers' own words*. Also, the beginning and end of each story is usually preceded and followed by our commentary, opinion and, hopefully, worthwhile insight. The full-length stories are never-before-published accounts acquired through phone, email, or face-to-face interviews with the experiencers. (One exception: "Night Terrors" from central Pennsylvania was emailed to us by the woman's grandson after she had passed away.) All names in all the related stories are fictitious, done to protect people's privacy. The chapters that are the authors' own first-hand encounters are signed with our names after the title and written in the first-person. We take full responsibility for the content of those stories.

In about the middle of each section of the book there is a collection of "Very Short Stories," each set in a different town in that area of the state. We include these to give the reader a break from the short-story pattern. And while we only used a dozen or so of the "shorts" in each section, we were supplied with enough of these to fill the entire book! These blurbs were provided to us courtesy of The International UFO Museum and Research Center in Roswell, New Mexico, but the accounts have been re-written to make them our own.

Keep in mind, as we have during our construction of this book, that anyone can be fooled at any time. We do not believe that has happened with *UFOs Above Pennsylvania*. We stand firm that the tales are true. The stories you are about to read were told by people with a passion—a burning motivation to make known an event in their lives that may never have been appreciated before by their circle of family, friends, or acquaintances. And for someone not to be heard, particularly regarding a topic one is connected to at a deep level, is a heart-shearing thrust, leaving a pain that can last for decades. Maybe now, with this book, for at least a few of the people, some of the pains have eased.

Lastly, and perhaps most important, it has been our pleasure to have communicated with those who are UFO and alien witnesses, whose lives can only be considered miraculous. Their spirits, and sometimes bodies, have been touched by other worlds. These people, spanning the last fifty years or so, have quietly escorted the next age of human existence to the front of the line. Beyond the Age of Enlightenment, beyond the Industrial Revolution, beyond the Space and Information Ages, with the experiencer's help, we begin The Age of Visitation.

~Gerard J. Medvec

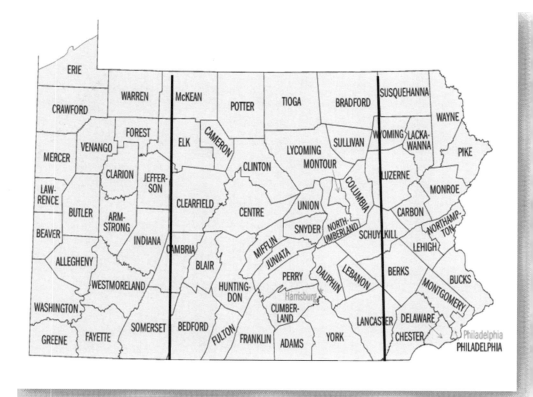

WESTERN   CENTRAL   EASTERN

Map of Pennsylvania sections.

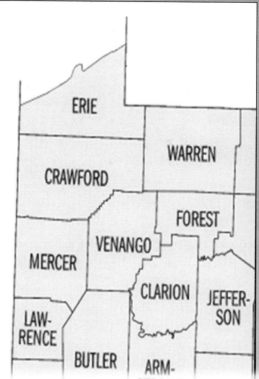

Western Pennsylvania

WESTERN

Chapter 1.
Deus Ex Machina
Greenville, Mercer County

Remember, you are just an extra in everyone else's play.
~*Franklin D. Roosevelt*
32nd President

Bill's psyche juggled the bizarre images like a drunken harlequin, trying to understand his place in the brief, massive theatre production being run by an alien race. He had been catapulted out of time and place, away from everything that was small-town Greenville.

Greenville, Pennsylvania marched into the twentieth century known for its railroad shops, bridge works, gristmills, a cement-block plant, an automobile factory, foundries and machine shops, saw and flour mills. Water power for these ventures was supplied by the Shenango River. In 1900, 4,814 people enjoyed the country setting next to the heavy industry in Greenville. By 2000, the census showed 6,380 folk. But the big-time manufacturing jobs had all but vanished. Today, the small town boasts a community

theatre, three museums, and Thiel College.

Bill was eleven years old in 1974. His family owned a small farm outside of rural Greenville. He had a pleasant childhood, worked at his chores when he wasn't in school, loved to hunt and fish, and reveled in running around the 150-acres when there was nothing else pending.

About an eighth of a mile from the farmhouse was the family junk yard. There was no trash pick-up for the small community in 1974, so rubbish was dumped at the rear of the property near the top of a steep ravine.

Bill's friend, Sammy, lived on a nearby farm. On the night of June 20, 1974, the night of a new moon, Sammy called and suggested, since there would be no moon that night, why didn't they go to Bill's junk yard and throw bottles into the ravine as they'd done many times before. They loved hearing them smash on the rocks in the dark; a game of judgment since the creek was about twenty-five to thirty feet down, and they couldn't see the rocks.

Around 9:30 that calm summer night the boys headed past the apple orchard and up the cow pasture to the edge of the ravine. There, a forest started. Behind them was a large wheat field. The glass bottle search began, with the subsequent bombardment of the invisible enemy rocks near the creek below. Bill was playing the part of a bomber pilot, or artillery gunner. Time whisked by. It was about 11:00. More bombs were needed so another bottle hunt began. While they searched, a high-pitched, swirling noise became audible. It quickly grew from faint to formidable. Bill and Sammy stopped their bottle-gathering.

"Do you hear that?" Bill asked.

"I do, but…" Sammy started.

A bright light began to illuminate the ground around them from above and behind, a' la Broadway spotlight. They turned to look.

"What the heck is that?" Bill asked. Before Sammy could open his mouth, the light blasted their eyes with an intensity that burned like hot coals. Bill couldn't see anything around him. Water streamed from throbbing tear ducts. The boys' bodies shook with terror; anxiety was up a hundred percent. The beam had hit them with a near-physical impact.

Bill knew the general direction of his house, so he started running, still unable to see, fear leading the way. Three steps later, he hit the electric cattle fence, which he had forgotten about, bounced off from the shock, and was slammed to the grass. He covered his head with his hands and arms, fighting off the light, blocking every entrance into his orifices. All around him was a loud, rumbling, booming noise. It was like the discordant bass section of an orchestra and an 8.9 earthquake were shoved into his ears at the same time

The air of the formerly calm summer night had launched into hurricane status. The pressure from the swooshing, popping wind that churned around him was so intense it gave Bill's body partial buoyancy. The light above still blinded and seared his eyes. But his curiosity craved an answer. He forced himself to look at the light, and as he did, it condensed in on itself, shrunk to a smaller diameter; then like lightning, burst upward and disappeared into the stars.

Remains of the junk yard, greatly cleaned-up since time of abduction. Only about 150 yards behind the house.

The boys were returned to earth near the tall, naked tree in the foreground on the right. The electric fence they ran into is at the center.

Bill's knees thumped together with the quick rhythm of a drum. Every nerve felt like its fleshy casing had been scraped off with a knife, and the ends tied together wrongly, making his insides a total short-circuit. He got a grip on himself; he stood up but was unable to see well because his eyes were filled with a residual fiery brightness. He rubbed his face and was grasping at the elusive control of his senses, when he heard "*zip, zip, zip.*" His eyes cleared.

Sammy had been right behind him and had also found the electric fence. But Sammy was older and taller than Bill. Instead of bouncing off the hot wire, he hit it waist-high and folded over it taking shock after shock. *Zip, zip, zip!* Bill latched on to the back of his friend's pants and shirt and yanked him to the ground. Sammy was unconscious.

"Sammy, Sammy, wake up. C'mon. We gotta get outa here!" Bill slapped and shook his friend until he revived.

"Where am…" Sammy started. His partially glazed eyes read total fright as he wobbled to upright. Bill knew there was no time for questions.

"Just run!" Bill shouted, and they fled toward the safety of Bill's home. Moments later the back door of the house burst open and the boys stumbled inside.

"Mom, Dad!" The boys were in hysterics. They told Bill's mother what had happened. While the story sounded completely fantastic, she recognized sincerity when she saw it. She looked outside, knowing that there was something out there that scrambled the boys' brain matter into useless jelly. But all she saw was a normal Pennsylvania summer night that was now over for the two adventurers.

During the next few months, Bill and Sammy would sit at the picnic table behind Bill's house, going over and over the "light from the sky" incident, and watch the heavens for a re-visit. Not that they wanted to be terrorized again; they were content without the intrusion of wild lights and horrific din. They *did* want to calm their curiosity that burned to know what happened on the stage of their lives that night.

Sammy's family moved away a couple years later, but returned to the area when Bill was a senior in high school. Bill grabbed his old friend one day.

"Do you remember that night?" he asked Sammy.

"When the light came down and scared the behoozzes out of us? I can't forget it," Sammy said as he looked slightly upward. Bill looked too, his eyes deepening with the lesson of an experience few people could appreciate.

It wasn't long before Sammy's family moved away again and the friends lost touch.

Recurring nightmares began to plague Bill during his college years. These dreams felt somehow connected to the "night of the bright light." Three times or more a month, the common, unpleasant theme was a dark shape that entered his dream and ignited a fear in him that became volcanic. He would struggle to wake, to end the terror, but sleep paralysis often blocked his efforts, allowing the dark form to loom ever longer, ever closer. He grappled with the fright and through mammoth effort would finally muster a piercing scream, which would jolt him past the paralysis and into consciousness, banishing the dark form from his exhausted mind.

After college, Bill married. The bad dreams, however, followed him into matrimony. Sometimes his new wife would aid in his nocturnal rescue by shaking him out of his panic-strewn visions. The numerous nightmares were disrupting the sleep patterns of the couple. Finally, Bill's wife suggested that he try hypnotherapy. She worked for the Worker's Bureau of Compensation in Ohio and said she knew a woman through her work who was a professional hypnotist. Apparently the therapist had helped various workers with physical and emotional issues, and also worked with police to regress witnesses to discover and refine details about crime scenes. Perhaps she could help Bill. Maybe he could be regressed to find out exactly what happened that night.

Bill always suspected that more happened than he could remember, but he had had no clue about how to unravel the mystery. However, he had always heard that hypnotism was a stage act; there was nothing scientific about it. Still, he kept an open mind. It would be interesting to meet this woman and learn if hypnotism was real or not.

It was now 1990. Bill and his wife had moved to East Liverpool, Ohio. The hypnotist lived in Youngstown, Ohio. The first session at her house was "cool," different, and a little exciting for Bill. Maybe an answer was ultimately imminent. The therapist showed Bill to her office and explained the deep state of relaxation that was hypnosis. It enabled a person to explore their mind and subconscious, she noted; looking inward rather than outward. This often allowed people to find information locked in a forgotten storeroom of their mind.

Bill sat in a plush, comfy chair in the office. Curtains were pulled shut for softer lighting, and she began the relaxation process. She instructed Bill to close his eyes and imagine he was walking down a flight of stairs. He was told to count backwards with each step down from ten to one. With each step he realized that he was going deeper into his subconscious mind. At the bottom of the stairs was a door. He went through the door in his mind. It was a comfortable, homey room. There was TV and a library. The library consisted of video tapes, each marked with a year. The therapist told Bill to take the 1974 tape off the shelf and slip it into the player near the TV. He was to pick up the imaginary remote control, lay back on the lounge, and be in complete control of all the events that would be reviewed this night. Start, stop, reverse, fast-forward — all were in his charge.

Initially, Bill was fascinated by this pleasant process. If the therapist hadn't been verbally leading the way, he could have dropped into dreamland. On he went to the summer of 1974. He immediately fast-forwarded to Sammy calling him and their decision to meet at Bill's, go to the junk yard, and throw bottles into the ravine. Bits of surprising detail surfaced to his mind: Sammy's loud knock on the back door, the All-Star Converse tennis shoes with the red star Bill was wearing, plus his blue jeans and Adidas t-shirt. He was cogni-zant of his surroundings and what he was doing. He was impressed with hypnotism. He saw details that would never otherwise be re-membered. Bill watched as he and Sammy walked through the mem-ory of his parent's apple orchard, picking up the fruit and tossing it at trees. Then they arrived at the junk yard.

There was a noise from above and behind. Bill watched himself turn to see the memory of the light in the sky. Suddenly, he felt like he was tied into an electric chair facing a stage full of strobe lights and loud speakers. At the moment he saw the light, somebody, somewhere, flipped a switch and Bill's body twitched like it was in a clonic seizure. His body was bombarded with the strobe lights and a monstrous noise. It was all happening again and *it felt just as real as the first time*, even though he was now under hypnosis. For the next few minutes, his only awareness was this punishment.

The therapist's voice began to seep through the torture. She was yelling, but sounded miles away. She grew louder.

"Bill, wake up. Come out of it! You are in control. Come out now!!"

Bill focused on the stressed female voice, as his muscles con-tracted and relaxed in rapid suc-cession, bouncing him up and down in the chair like a teddy bear. At last the convulsions subsided, the lights dimmed, the violent noises muffled. Bill pried his eyes open. The large head of the therapist was almost in his face, which dripped on all sides with perspiration.

"What the hell just happened?" he pushed the question through his fatigue.

"You had me scared for a while," she answered as she straightened up, regaining professionalism, but continued to study Bill's face. "I'm not sure what happened. In my twenty years doing this, I've never seen such violent reaction under hypnotic regression."

"Well there must be some explanation," Bill insisted.

"In some cases, people revivify, that is, they relive experiences from the past. Maybe that's what happened."

"I need more than 'maybe'. I've always felt that more had happened that night than seeing the burning light and hearing that racket."

"There is another possibility." The therapist turned paler.

"A good one, I hope," Bill wished.

The woman retreated from Bill and flopped in her chair. "Sometimes," she started, "a person goes through such a horrifying, traumatic episode that their subconscious absolutely does not want them to recall the event—ever. So, rather than let you see those images again, your brain fired off all its synapses to prevent you from seeing or knowing what happened."

Bill found all of these explanations disturbing. "What do we do now?" He was frustrated, without an answer.

"It's up to you. If you want to proceed, I'll give you a series of exercises you can practice in a quiet place at home. Once mastered, you'll be in control of what you see, and how you feel and react to the information in the next session. But I won't do another session unless you study these relaxation exercises first. Hopefully, there will be no convulsions. I also want to have my mentor, a PHD from Case Western Reserve University, observe the session. I'll contact him, with your permission, and see what he says. Frankly, Bill, a lot of this is beginning to sound like alien abduction."

"Oh," Bill said a little too quietly, since his mind told him to laugh. His heart, however, quivered as if he'd just been offered the starring role in his own life's story.

"The doctor has worked in the government and has had many dealings with the abduction scenario," she assured him as she wrote a note to herself to call her mentor.

"I'm too curious about this missing part of my life. I must find out what happened. I'm not giving up now. I don't care if you invite Oprah Winfrey."

Over the next four months, Bill practiced the relaxation and control exercises the hypnotherapist had given him. Initially, it took hours to get through the program. But after a couple months, and with great effort, he had wheedled the time down to half an hour. A date for a second session was picked, and the therapist said that the doctor from CWRU would attend as an observer only. He would not get involved unless there was an "emergency."

Bill agreed to these parameters for his second hypnotic session. At this point he decided to find Sammy. He wanted to corroborate this experience with his old friend. Would Sammy be interested in being regressed? Bill did not want to bias him, so he would tell him nothing about his first session, or the therapist's mentioning of anything alien. He wanted a pure comparison. He needed to trust the answers. It would be important if they both divulged the same story through hypnotism. Bill believed this was the only way to find out what really happened that summer night.

He called his parents and asked if they were still in touch with Sammy's parents. They were not, but they had ideas about where to find them. Once contact was made with Sammy's family, however, they sadly learned that Sammy had passed away a couple years prior from a heart condition. Bill would have to act out the rest of the scene without his old friend.

Bill's second drive to Youngstown was a traffic jam of doubt. He already knew from research that strange things could happen while under hypnosis. His own first attempt proved that. Would he be able to stay in control? He had worked hard on the relaxation exercises; yet doing them alone in a quiet room of his own house would be different than doing them on cue in a professional's office with strangers watching. Would he be able to maintain the discipline of self-control throughout the session? And what would be learned? Were the answers to be, or not to be, true? Would his feelings and need for closure taint the results with self-inflicted delusion? Needing to know what happened that night outweighed all doubts and possible foul-ups. The stage was set for act two.

The therapist and the doctor were waiting for him. The doc introduced himself and essentially said he was there to observe only, unless something went wrong, which it wouldn't. He said he was skilled in all forms of hypnotism, including returning people safely from mental precipices. But he would not interfere unless asked to by Bill or the therapist. Bill was glad to meet him, and after the wild first session, was glad he was there as backup. Bill had decided to video tape the session more as evidence for himself in case he had a seizure, rather than for any UFO issue and the therapist had agreed.

He took his place in the recliner and went through the relaxation process with the therapist. Deeper and deeper into his subconscious he traveled, reviewing the events he saw in his mind's eye that happened in 1974. He was again amazed over the fine details that came to life. Like throwing the apples at a tree—he'd missed the first throw, hit the second. Bill was back at the junk yard, picking up bottles, throwing them down onto the rock near the creek. He could hear them shatter. It was the same as real.

The high-pitched whirring noise returned. Then the light dropped out of the sky, blindingly fast and blindingly bright. He was paralyzed with fear, and sightless. Bill had been sharing these details out loud with the two therapists. But with the sudden paralysis, he stopped talking.

"Bill, are you all right? What do you see?" The therapist continued asking for responses.

Bill kicked himself past the numbness in his body and began to describe the new, frightful visions. He became engulfed in a bluish-white bubble of haze. There was the sensation of floating towards the light. He knew he was no longer on the ground. Then everything blacked out.

The next moment, Bill was in a room. It felt dome shaped and devoid of details. There was a gray mist all around. He struggled to understand. The feelings of where he was and what was around him continued to confuse his mind. He realized he was lying on a smooth, hard surface and that he had no clothes on. He fought to grasp why. Gray shapes, like in his nightmares, were to the side, in his peripheral vision. This terrified him unlike any fear he'd ever experienced before, but he still didn't know why. It was just a gray shape, nothing specific. He heard the therapist say to focus on the shape. He did.

Wherever he was, he was in a purplish bubble that had a barrier a few inches in front of his face. When he realized that, he understood the barrier made everything beyond it appear distorted, hard to see. He pressed his focus beyond the barrier.

When he did, the gray shape came to his right side. He saw a being with very thin arms, legs, and torso, and a large triangular-shaped head. Bill's nerves felt like they'd been put on an anvil and pounded with a mace. He saw the huge, almond-shaped, nauseating black eyes as being empty of all emotion. The shape was standing over him looking down. His body trembled as if in an earthquake. The being reached in through the bubble, holding a metallic, pointed instrument with what looked like a fiber-optic cable attached to the back that stretched to the ceiling and disappeared. It touched different parts of his body with this device. Wherever it touched, it pinched and burned slightly, and pulled at the skin. Then another gray shape came to his left side and repeated the process.

The gray beings then walked away. As he looked around, about ten feet to his right, he saw Sammy lying naked on a similar table, encased in a bluish bubble. They did the same thing to him.

During this session, Bill's pinky fingers were gyrating in odd ways.

"What is going on with those fingers, Bill," the therapist asked.

Bill directed his focus through the haze to his smallest digits. There were metallic thimbles attached to his pinky toes and fingers, each with another fiber optic-like cable attached, and that cable was hanging from somewhere in a gray mist overhead. There was a constant tingling sensation at each connection.

The next thing he heard was a chattering noise. He couldn't understand where it was coming from, so he focused his attention and learned *he* was making the sound. His teeth chattered. The table under him was frigid.

Then everything went black again.

The next sensation was something familiar. His hands were kneading and digging into it. It was grass. There was a loud whirring sound, then a pop. The light was again burning his eyes. Then, as he forced a look into it, the light collapsed on itself and streaked back into the night sky and disappeared.

He got up, grabbed Sammy off the electric fence, revived him, and they fled back to his house.

The therapist reversed Bill through the relaxation process and brought him safely out of hypnosis. The session was over.

Afterwards, the doctor put his hands on Bill's shoulders. "Bill, I kind of envy you. You're embarking on a journey that few of us will understand and fewer still will ever participate in."

Too exhausted to ask at the time, Bill often wondered why the man spoke in present tense. Bill continues to wrestle with emotions over this show-stopping life event. He is still conflicted about what comes out under hypnosis: Is it real or not? Did he obsess too much over the years about the summer night in 1974? Had his mind simply created a fantasy story to fill in the blanks? Had he fooled himself? He wishes he could remember these things outside of the hypnotherapy session. But he cannot — not like he can remember his college graduation, for instance. He is sure that under hypnosis he did not lie, twist, or contort anything.

Abduction stories are not new, although this story has never before been published. So prevalent are they that they've become part of our recent history. These remarkable stories, as brought to light by researchers like the late Budd Hopkins and the late John Mack, M.D., have forever changed our perception of who we are in the Universe. Like it or not, we are not at the top of the food chain. As the Universe continues expanding and growing older, with the potential for infinite varieties of life forms, our lives are playing out on an ever-shrinking stage. For Bill, he may wonder if, before his final curtain, the climactic scene in his story has already been played? Like the ancient Greek tragedies and comedies, maybe at critical times in all our lives, the paths we choose are actually chosen for us by a god-like being parked far away in his machine.

Chapter 2

The Hunted
Greenville, Mercer County

They have a tendency to root for the fugitive.
They're always on the side of the animal being chased.
~Norman Jewison
Canadian film director/producer

Two common conditions of humanity are: the survival of the fittest and the pecking order. It seems that aliens do not follow these guidelines; not usually.

Bill was a senior in high school in February of 1981. He had just bought a new electronic fox call—that is, a rabbit-in-distress call. His friend, Luke, also from Greenville, Pennsylvania, and he, wanted to test it. They decided to hunt for fox at the back of Bill's parent's 150-acre farm. Luke got to Bill's house around 11 p.m. on a cold, clear night. Foxes are active at night, so the boys felt that being set to hunt by midnight would be the perfect time. They packed guns and ammo into Bill's truck and drove along the edge of the family property into the woods on a logging road cut by Bill and his grandfather. They followed the ravine for about two miles further.

Their destination was a thick, acre-sized briar patch on the far side of the ravine. This was the perfect spot for foxes to den. It was impossible for humans or large animals to move through it to threaten their home. When they neared the crossover spot, they parked the truck, gathered their gear, and took their new fox call through the woods down one side of the ravine and up the other to the briar patch. Their rifles were scoped with red lenses so the foxes' eyes would glow red in the sights, making them easier to see at night. Just inside the patch, the fox call was set and activated. Standing off the trail a few feet, with the briar patch on the right and creek on the left, the boys grew silent. They waited.

Only four or five minutes later, red eyes appeared on the trail. A fox had heard the call. Foxes typically stalk in concentric circles around their prey before attacking, and that's what this fox tried to do. A wide circle was made first. Then a smaller one. The fox neared the edge of the ravine.

Guns fired. A hit. But the impact shoved the fox over the edge and rolled it down toward the creek. Both boys hurriedly grabbed their equipment, jogged to where the body had flown over the edge, and stumbled down the hill to collect their prize.

"That new call works good," Luke noted.

"We were lucky the fox was nearby," Bill replied, feeling a little disquieted for a hunter who had just helped to take down a target with one shot. "Almost too easy."

But at the creek they couldn't find the fox. Then they heard it panting and clawing away a few yards ahead, dragging itself through the brush back up the hill. They rushed towards it. Thinking it would reach the briar patch first and disappear in the bramble, they hurried back up the hill to cut off its retreat. At the top of the ravine, they were about twelve yards from the patch. They turned to watch the ground, waiting for the fox to climb over the edge so they could put it down.

The night was clear, beautiful. Bill was aware of the sounds of darkness filling his ears as they waited. Dogs barked in the distance, frogs croaked, insects cricketed, and the wind pressed his face, all keeping the world alive.

Then in one heart-beat...dead silence. Every sound they'd been listening to ceased. Every cricket, every dog, every frog within miles, in the same moment, stopped making noise. It was as if the world had shut down.

Bill and Luke looked at each other and didn't need to say: "What's going on here?" Nerves in both their bodies were plucked. Without warning, a light appeared in the middle of the briar, a strange light. It was basketball size, but not three-dimensional; two-dimensional only. It resembled a light you saw through water-soaked eyes. The edges were frayed with jagged light-spikes.

Fear rose in the boys like zombies from a grave. There was no explanation for a light to appear in the middle of the field.

"Maybe there is someone out there hunting with a carbide lantern on their head," Bill said.

They started hollering, "Hey, anybody out there? Anybody there?"

No sound. Knots in their stomachs turned tighter. Bill pumped his rifle with a few rounds of ammo and shouted, "You better answer or we're gonna shoot. By the count of three."

Still silence.

"One…"

Both hunters hoped for a human response.

"Two…"

Could this be someone hunting them? Why was there no response from a responsible fellow hunter?

"Three!"

Bill fired three times into the air.

The light turned off for a second, then relit. It began moving towards the boys, flying slowly over the briar patch. Icy pin pricks of fear formed on their spinal columns. Bill was paralyzed with terror.

"Oh my god, it's coming for us," he thought. He wanted to move away from it. He wanted to grab Luke and run. But he couldn't move in any direction. He couldn't even raise his gun for protection. He wasn't sure what Luke's condition was, but he didn't see him moving either. What to do?

The fuzzy light came out of the briar patch about twenty yards from the fox trackers and stopped behind a big oak tree along the road. The light was about three feet off the ground. It sparkled and shimmered. Around the edge were small spikes of various lengths. It resembled a cartoon sun in shape, a real sun in intensity. When it stopped behind the tree, it did not illuminate the tree or the surroundings. Occasionally a spark would fly off one of the pointed ends. It made no sound. In the all-encompassing silence, the only sound to be heard was the boys' ragged breaths.

After what seemed like an ice age, it came out from behind the tree, continued down the edge of the ravine, away from the petrified hunters, into the woods and out of sight.

Once it was gone, the boys flung their equipment in all directions and sprinted to the truck, barreled to Bill's house, and called Luke's dad on the phone. (Bill's parents were not home.) Luke's dad arrived after only minutes, chided the "kids" for leaving the equipment up the hill, since he didn't believe their story, and drove them to the "scene of the crime." They hoped at least to get the fox along with their guns and bags. But all traces of the fox, and the flat, circular, pointy-edged light, were gone. The night was noisy again, bursting with the sounds of nature. The hunt was over.

Chapter 3.
A Few Very Short Stories

A collection of short descriptions of sightings—courtesy of International UFO Museum and Research Center, Roswell, New Mexico; The National UFO Reporting Center (www.ufocenter.com); and Filer's Files.com.

Butler County
June 16, 2010;
approximately 11 p.m.

A person witnessed six jet fighters chase a blinding white spherical light in the skies over his home. While the object moved continuously, it did achieve short bursts of speed to keep ahead of the fighters.

Canonsburg,
Washington County
January 12, 2008;
approximately 6 p.m.

Five people (three in a car and two strangers at a nearby parking lot) saw a flying triangle. The car had been heading north on Pike Street towards Route 980. While stopped at that intersection, a large white light appeared over the traffic light, a fair distance away, and was traveling directly towards the witnesses. The object flew over them. On the bottom of the triangle was a large center light surrounded by three smaller red lights. The object had the appearance of being "see through." Two other witnesses were in a parking lot near the intersection pointing up at the triangle.

East Springfield, Erie County
December 12, 2005;
approximately 9:30 p.m.

While driving south on a local road, the witness

saw a bright blue-white, two-foot diameter ball of light. It hovered close to the ground.

Greensburg, Westmoreland County
November 16, 2009; approximately 3 p.m.

Going west on Route 30 near the Mountain View Inn, the witness saw "two birds" fighting each other over the highway. Upon a closer look, these were not birds, but five-pointed star-shaped objects. They were spinning, rotating, and circling each other. Circular, ringed ridges were on the bodies emanating from the center point outwards. They were flying close to the tree tops. The backs of the crafts each had a giant red light about three feet in height and six feet in length, with vertical rows of additional lights that would flash. When the objects moved away, they were unsteady, wobbling, and tilting from side-to-side.

Grove City, Mercer County
April 4, 2007; approximately 3:10 a.m.

While star-watching from their roof, two witnesses saw a boomerang-shaped object appear just below the clouds, making no sound at all. It was a gold-rimmed, shadowy craft about the size of a car.

Indiana County
November 20, 2006; approximately 4:30 p.m.

While walking through a field, the witness saw a fast-moving, blimp-like shape in the sky about a quarter mile away. It hovered low near the field for three to four minutes, then departed.

Lake Erie
June 14, 2009; time unknown.

While fishing on the lake, the witness spotted a bright star-like object flying close to a jet plane, moving parallel with the jet without a contrail. This continued about thirty seconds when the object stopped in mid-air for ten seconds, then changed course at an angle and flew three-quarters of the way to the northern horizon of the lake where it stopped again. Suddenly it moved at amazing speed back towards the west where it slowed again, stopped, then headed north, and was gone.

McKeesport, Allegheny County
March 28, 2008;
approximately 10:20 p.m.

Four unusual craft came east. They were flying low and without any noise. The craft did not follow any normal flight patterns. Each had one red light on the top in addition to flashing and static lights. They were heading east, then swerved north and flew away. They circled back around, then continued to fly in a circle. After about fifteen minutes, they flew off in a northwest direction.

New Kensington,
Westmoreland County
November 17, 2009;
approximately 6:01 p.m.

The witness was driving, when he observed a bright light in the distance. He drove to the top of Coxcomb Hill. The light was actually a craft, disc-shaped, with a glowing white light with a blue tint on the bottom center. It was at least 1,000 feet up. Upon getting closer, the witness realized the disc shape was only the center part of a larger, triangular-shaped vessel. There were lights at each corner. The object moved with increasing speed towards Plum Township, then was gone.

Pittsburgh, Allegheny County
April 6, 2007;
approximately 11:15 p.m.

Three witnesses were driving by the lake, when on the opposite side they saw two high beams shining at them. There was no road on the opposite side, however, for a car to traverse. It was not a helicopter because there was no sound. The high beams suddenly took off and moved over the trees away from the witnesses' position. It was about 200 yards away, bigger than a streetlight and not part of a larger object. It then turned from white to a darker amber shade, but the light did not illuminate anything. The object moved slowly below the tree line, back up, then slowly away until it disappeared.

Warren, Warren County July 8, 2011; approximately 9:17 p.m.

On the Alleghany River, the witness was fishing when he noticed a UFO over the refinery across the river. He flashed his LED flashlight at the object to make it aware he was watching. The object moved slowly for about two minutes, then accelerated and was gone. Five minutes later, it popped into the atmosphere above him, then was gone again. At 9:30 p.m., he saw two stars coming into view. The right star moved to the right. Another UFO again appeared above his boat, hovering at about 1,000 feet. He fired his flashlight at it. The object descended to within 200 feet—then flashed its lights at the witness. The craft then accelerated upward and was gone.

West Springfield, Erie County March 8, 2011; approximately 8 p.m.

Three lights appeared in the sky above a horse farm about one mile from Lake Erie. Two witnesses said the lights were about fifty feet apart. The shape was boomerang-like. Its lights were light blue and yellow-green. The boomerang was over the correctional facility, which had a no-fly zone under 500 feet. The UFO was much lower. It flew vertically and moved north, then disappeared.

Chapter 4.
Something Different in a Lifetime
Beaver Falls, Beaver County

We may have all come on different ships, but we're in the same boat now.
~Dr. Martin Luther King, Jr.
Civil rights leader

The music shop was closed. Nobody had called to cancel Walt's guitar lesson—this was rude and unusual. His dad was acting a bit peeved that he had driven his son the couple of miles to get there for no reason.

But there was a reason.

The cold, northwestern Pennsylvania, November day in 1967 was sunny and bright. The heater in the two-year-old Chevy station wagon with the wood paneling, sounded like a propeller in a wind tunnel. Walt and his dad were headed down Concord Circle Road returning home. As they crested the road, twelve-year-old Walt spotted a large, near neutral gray, solid, long-nosed triangular-shaped craft hovering directly over the street in front of their house. It was about 1,000 feet up, sported a bright light in each corner, and was totally quiet.

"Why is it over my house?" Walt's dad mumbled at first glimpse of the strange sight. The Second World War former O.S.S. agent, who was stationed behind the lines in Burma, immediately had misgivings about the flying object. He had heard talk about them during the war, but he'd never expected one to be perched just off his front porch in Beaver Falls.

Walt grew quiet. He wasn't sure if seeing this different looking object was good or bad. His eyes volleyed back and forth from craft to dad, waiting to see what emotions to mimic.

To activate a lighter feeling in the car, his dad said, "I wonder if there's a bunch of girls in there coming to pick me up." He smiled broadly at Walt.

Walt cracked a smile back, glad that his father wasn't falling into a suspicious spy-mode.

The car crawled down the hill, the driver riding the brake. He turned right into his driveway, under the shadow of the UFO, and rolled to the back of the house. The triangle made no movement, perhaps waiting for new orders, or perhaps just waiting.

While his dad hurried through the kitchen door, Walt ran right to the open side porch where he had a perfect view of the machine overhead. The wood railing warmed quickly as his small hands tightened on the hand rail.

His dad herded his mom and three sisters excitedly onto the wood porch. "Come on, come on. I want to show you something. Everybody outside. I want you to see this. It's something different in our lifetime," his dad said with a smile, as he pointed to an empty heaven. It was gone.

"Dad, it left really fast," Walt said with childhood verve. Nothing he'd ever seen had ever moved that fast. This was no balloon or neighbor's kite. Young Walt knew it was intelligently controlled. When the device left, there was no starting up, no smoke, nothing that every combustion engine in the world would have to do. It was just gone. It took two seconds to angle itself upwards towards space. In two seconds, it had traversed the visible sky and evaporated into the upper atmosphere. And in those two seconds, it had burned itself into Walt's memory forever.

The next day, Walt was watching *The Man from U.N.C.L.E.* TV series. Suddenly, his head jerked backwards in a "what the heck?" moment. "Dad, Dad! Hurry, look at this!"

His dad hurried into the room. On the TV, a similar, black triangle vehicle was displayed on the show as part of the story. Walt and his dad were fascinated at the coincidence, but it wasn't the same thing. The TV triangle had sides made out of round tubes and the center of the triangle was an open space. The one over the house was solid all-around and flat on the bottom.

"That's what we saw yesterday," his dad asserted with only half conviction.

Walt knew the difference from the fake image on TV and the real image that hung in the air near his house the day before. He was sure that, in the back of his dad's mind, maybe someone in the UFO was coming to get them. Maybe it was from the Air Force, a spying device checking on a former O.S.S. agent. But Walt, even as a child, knew it wasn't. The UFO hovered without the slightest movement. Planes, jets, even helicopters cannot do that. They were always moving one way or the other.

"No it wasn't," Walt responded with a sly smile. He knew his dad was trying to trick him, or something.

The possibility that a UFO came by his house to make its presence known has been a cherished memory and an inspiration for Walt. While his religion is unclear on alien beings, he feels that such a vast universe has to have more than one measly planet with living beings on it. It's different to consider that other beings inhabit the Universe. And different is good.

Chapter 5.
One Will Get You Three
Albion, Erie County

**Life, like poker, has an element of risk.
It shouldn't be avoided. It should be faced.**
~Edward Norton
Actor

Joe flipped the cards across the blanket like a casino shark. There was nobody on the other side to receive them, however, which was good, since the two-person, backyard tent barely allowed room for the thirteen-year-old Joe.

It was a June night in 1985, predictably warm, but with enticing clear skies over the small borough of Albion, Pennsylvania. The stars looked like a thousand pin pricks on a black canvas, backlit by heavenly grace. It was anyone's bet how many of the bright dots in the sky were actually UFOs.

Joe's one-man poker game was going well. He stayed polite when he won, took it well when he lost. That was until around ten o'clock, when his mom called from the kitchen door that he shouldn't stay up all night and that the door would be unlocked in case he needed the restroom.

Joe put away his cards, nestled into the sleeping bag, and tried to let go of the million-dollar pot he had pretended he had just won in Atlantic City.

For a half hour, he tossed and flipped. No comfortable position could be found on the bumpy backyard grass. Then something told him to check out the stars. He unstuffed himself out of the sleeping bag, ducked through the tent's door flap, shuffled into the sweet summer air, and looked up.

The distant suns were gorgeous. But there was one big, bright light that didn't seem to belong. It was too big. It was standard star color, and was perfectly round, but seemed to be wobbling slightly from side to side, like a picture dangling from a short string. The object hung several degrees above the tallest trees at the back of the family property.

Joe could feel its intelligence.

And that it was ogling him.

The two stared at each other across the unknown. One from outer space was betting, perhaps, that the boy would run. One from planet Earth was betting that the giant, lighted object was the most amazing thing he had ever seen. Who would play their hand first?

The deadlock went on for about thirty seconds.

All of a sudden, the light broke into three equal, smaller pieces. The pieces, still glowing bright, only smaller, moved away from each other at the same angle: 120 degrees, a feat unlikely to happen in nature. They traveled, not at the usual UFO breakneck speeds, but at a casual saunter. They were the same color as the original craft. With no human objects nearby in the sky, Joe could not determine the real size and distance of the lights. He just knew they were fantastic, better than fireworks, and from far away. He kept track of each one, visually checking its trajectory, speed, and angle, confirming in his youthful mind as much of the scientific data as he could collect. He couldn't wait to tell everyone: his mom and dad, his friends at school, the science teacher.

The three UFOs, remaining true to their original paths, finally disappeared behind trees to the left and right, and over the far horizon of the clear summer sky. The night was normal again.

Joe raced into the house to tell his mom. She listened carefully, asked him if it was gone—yes—then told him to use the restroom and go back to sleep. That was the last time it was brought up at home.

The next day, despite an enthusiastic telling of the incident, his friends were equally unimpressed with his "'imagination." (Joe decided then not to share his tale with any of the teachers, or anyone else at all until now.)

A short time later, Joe set aside the cards and went on to other things, more adult things, things that the average person could talk about. One thing that never changed though was his memory of the triple-splitting UFO that he'd faced alone, not only as a real experience on a June night as a young boy, but as an evocative memory during the few decades that followed.

Older and wiser, he now knows all the things that it was not, making it the only thing it could be. And—he got *three for the price of one.* Joe liked the odds.

Chapter 6.
Game Interrupted
Harrison Township, Allegheny County

**Rude contact with facts chased my
visions and dreams quickly away.**
~Victoria Woodhull
First woman to run for
President of the United States, 1872

A Harrison Township resident, eleven-year-old Greg was about to make his hook shoot towards the white plywood backboard nailed on the telephone pole. But his arm stopped in mid-throw. The basketball nose-dived halfway to the basket. His friends were about to jeer or cheer, depending on which team they were on, but the look on Greg's face stopped them.

Greg was looking almost directly overhead at something odd. Odd isn't tolerated well in western Pennsylvania.

You can't have a history of Harrison Township without tying it to its near neighbor, Pittsburgh. From colonial times and the construction of Fort Pitt to defend against Natives, French, or English, up to the pounding steel mills of Andrew Carnegie and the creation of U.S. Steel, Harrison Township and Allegheny County were at the forefront of expansionism across the continent, and across the Industrial Revolution. Harrison Township was formally organized as a first-class Township in March 1900. Most people know it as Natrona and Natrona Heights, but Harrison Township is the legal name. Today, the population is just over 10,000 occupies 7.2 square miles of land on the west shore of the Allegheny River, about 20 miles northeast of downtown Pittsburgh.

But what halted the street game had nothing to do with history or steel.

It was 1968, a warm late summer Friday night, around 8:30. Everybody was out on Meadow Street socializing with family or friends. It was a good neighborhood. People looked out for each other, listened to each other's problems, offered and accepted advice.

Meadow Street dead-ended. It had to since it ran straight into Pine Hill, a small protrusion of the Appalachians covered in trees. It was a favorite climbing spot, playground, and hangout for the local kids. The basketball game, about a block from the woods on Meadow, was going well. Greg had been intent on winning this game. His average for wins and losses was about 50/50. It would be fun busting out of the draw. But not that night.

Over the tree tops of Pine Hill suddenly appeared a round, flying object. The bottom had numerous red, yellow, and green lights near the outer edge, all of which seemed to rotate from clockwise to counter-clockwise and back again continuously. The lights were large, bright — not like engine running lights on a plane. And they were not headlights since they were on the bottom of the flying circle. It was dead silent. The circular device was about 200 feet in the air and flew slowly towards Greg and his friends.

The basketball boys jumped on their bicycles and shot off in different directions. Some went towards the object for a better look; some went left and right to tell the neighborhood about it. Greg shot away from the damn thing, heading home for cover. He didn't like the looks of it.

With the first pump of the pedals, his bike felt like it was buried in quicksand. But he pressed down harder and faster. He pulled at the handle bars like a weight-lifter going for a world record. It felt like hours were passing. The bike finally beat gravity and friction and shot him forward. As he raced on, he continually looked over his shoulder. Where was that flying saucer? With every look it was still there, keeping pace with him, following him home. It never occurred to a frightened eleven-year-old not to drag home a UFO. Dad might get angry. But Greg had no choice. Home was where the super-human fixer of all his problems lived — Mom.

Greg paced his bike faster than he had ever done. The neighbors marveled at the streak of the frightened child that flashed by. But when they saw him looking back, and followed his fearful gape, they too saw the flying oddity and forgot all else.

It was about a fifth of a mile to the project house, but to Greg it felt like five miles. The ship was still above him and felt like it was getting closer.

Finally, he hit his parent's front steps with his bike, jumped off, dropped the handle bars, and charged in the house. "Mom, there's a flying saucer chasing me!" he shouted with the seriousness that only an eleven year old could conjure for such an exclamation. He raced past his Dad who sat in his favorite chair reading the newspaper.

In the kitchen, his mom stopped in mid-chore and looked at her hard-breathing son. "What did you say?" She thought she heard right. But why would he say that?

"C'mon outside; I'll show you!"

Greg raced back out the front door. His Mom, wiping her hands on a dish towel, was right behind. His Dad scrambled from behind his newspaper, and not wanting to miss anything, bounced off the seat and pursued as well.

Dozens of people had filled the streets. Greg's friends had done a good job of informing the neighborhood of the high-flying, out-of-this-world visitor. People were pointing up at the brightly colored, circular mass.

"Will you look at that! What is it? I've never seen nothin' like that before. Must be a new type of helicopter, or plane, or somethin'."

The Harrison Township neighborhood was buzzing with the curious, the shocked, and the skeptical. By the end of the night it was decided: Nobody knew what it was.

All this time, the UFO had been hovering over the enthralled throng of people in their Pittsburgh suburb. After about ten minutes, at the same slow speed that it came, it left, heading back over Pine Hill, forever out of sight. This gave plenty of time for farewells—an oddity among UFO standard high-speed behavior.

The UFO had stopped the game and everything else on Meadow Street. Up until that night, Greg may have dreamed about spectacular hook shots, joining a pro basketball team, or just getting a good job at the steel mill. But since that night, the rude fact that UFOs exist may have deflated some of his earth-bound fantasies and carried his older and wiser dreams far into the Universe—to a clearer understanding.

Pine Hill today with Route 28 cutting through. UFO flew
over top of this hill towards Natrona Heights, which is
behind the camera and about sixty feet downhill.

Meadow Street, looking from near Greg's house towards dead-end where UFO first appeared. It then chased Greg back to this area.

Meadow Street. Telephone pole where backboard was hung. UFO flew over Pine Hill on left and came down towards this area, before following the street, and Greg, towards his house in the distance.

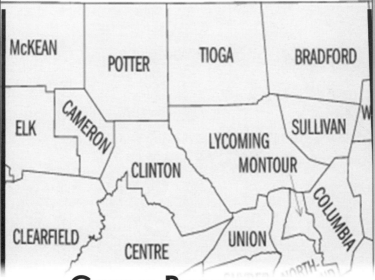

CENTRAL PENNSYLVANIA

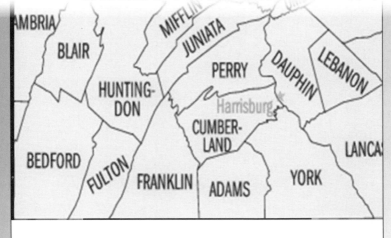

CENTRAL

Chapter 7.
The Following
Lebanon, Lebanon County

I felt like a hunted animal, followed constantly, waiting to be killed.
~Richard Jewell
Security guard involved with the Centennial Olympic Park bombing at the 1996 Summer Olympics in Atlanta, Georgia

Dave slid into the diner booth across from his friend, Jason, and was stunned in the next second. Jason's long arm pushed a white envelope with some writing on it across the table. He quickly rose from his seat.

"Don't follow me," Jason said with a black glare at Dave, as giant strides from his 6'3" frame propelled him towards and out the door.

"What the...," Dave started, as he realized the hour and a half ride up the Pennsylvania Turnpike to this monthly meeting with his friend was over before either said hello. This was a serious pain since he had plenty to do at his Lansdowne, Delaware County home; he would have liked a phone call before he left if there was a problem, since he also couldn't afford to waste gas.

He picked up the #10 envelope and read:

Dave Miller, act as if you don't know me; I'm being followed.

Dave looked around Gail's Diner and Gas Station on Route 72 just north of exit 20 of the turnpike. No ninjas, Navy seals, or Men-in-Black were ready to attack him. The diner was empty. A confused, irritated Dave ripped the envelope open and slipped out a two-page letter. He quickly peeled it apart to read. A five-dollar bill fell out.

Wednesday, 7/15/1998.

Dave,

Sorry to disappoint you, but we will not meet again for a while, probably months. I enjoyed our meetings about our paranormal experiences. I'll miss them. Here's what's happening.

When I called Mexico to talk to Jaime Maussan, the reporter who handled the April 6, 1997 Mexico City UFO sightings about the tapes I've made of UFOs around Lebanon, someone else must have been listening. My spirit guide confirmed this.

The UFO activity here has attracted those black helicopters; only now, they seem attracted to me. Yesterday, Tuesday the 14th, I took a walk near Stoever's Dam Park. A large, black, military helicopter flew over me, then hovered above me and shone a spotlight at me. I didn't know why and was confused at first, but then became suspicious.

At 5:30 p.m., while waiting in my car for my father outside of Walmart, they flew over me again, very low. Then at around 10 p.m. last night,

there was another flyover — at my house! It was so low I thought it was going to hit the roof.

Still intent on making copies of my videotapes of UFOs, I worked till about 5 a.m. taking a break around 3:45 a.m. When I glanced out my bedroom window, at the corner across the street was a tan, Ford Taurus. As soon as I peered through the mini-blinds, its lights flashed on and it raced away. Are you getting the picture? This is serious. They know who I am, where I live, and I'm sure they have placed a wiretap on my phone. I've never been so nervous and anxious.

Thank God I had an appointment this morning with my psychic. She was awesome and helped me channel some answers. I've been advised to put the tapes away for a year, and lay low. You should lay low, too. While I'm not afraid of our black helicopter "friends," I do consider my immediate position as extremely serious and dangerous.

I love you, pal! Remember our good times together. Nothing stays the same. I am not opposed to contact by mail. I will absolutely not discuss any of the above material by phone. Here's $5.00 for your trouble.

Good Luck!

Your friend,
Jason W. Wallbeck

Dave's insides went cold as his outside went damp. His mind was in a fast orbit around the sun. Could all this wildness be true? Over the past couple of months, Jason had been videotaping strange lights just outside Lebanon. The two friends reviewed the tapes as part of their monthly meeting. In these meetings, they would normally discuss the paranormal experiences each had during the previous thirty days. But over the last few months, the UFO topic became dominant in Jason's life. Viewing the UFO images on the camcorder's 2½" LED screen wasn't ideal, but it was all they had. They would meet for hours and speculate.

Jason's UFO hotspot was a middle school surrounded by plowed fields. While facing the building, on the left was a narrow strip of trees and bushes that guarded a short span of the school's property line. The trees were about fifty yards from the building. The next nearest buildings were on the farm about a half-mile across the field, so that the little copse seemed marooned on a thin line between dirt and grass. How Jason knew to drive to the school on certain nights at two o'clock in the morning to catch UFO "lights" was a mystery even to him. He just knew to do it. Despite a run-in with the police and a warning never to trespass on school grounds again, something urged him to return. Almost every time he did, there were "lights" near the strip of trees, which he videoed. He'd actually filmed the alien lights twice. What he captured on his camera were two lighted globes hovering near the ground, with what appeared to be a small, round, gray, metallic craft behind them. Sadly, because these items were on the other side of the strip of trees and bushes, it was never 100 percent clear in the video what they were. Jason wasn't interested in getting a closer shot. Safety kept him thirty-yards away.

On another night, something told Jason, again, to grab his video recorder around 1 a.m. and head for the side door of his home. The neighbor's house was only about ten yards away. There, between his single house and the neighbor's, was an alien globe. It was about soccer ball size, and awash in a soft glow of light. The globe meandered about five feet in the air from the front of the property to the back, between houses, and passing the side door without a care. This was a one-time event.

There were only three UFO incidents total that Jason had on video. This was the tape he wanted broadcast on Mexican television since the American media wouldn't touch it. The Mexican newsman, Jaime Maussan, who had covered a major sighting of UFOs over Mexico City in August 1997, was due to attend a convention in Roswell, New Mexico. Jason had phoned his studio in Mexico, talked to him briefly about his prized tape, and was told to call the newsman a few days later at the Holiday Inn in Roswell. Jason agreed to send him the tape, then over-nighted a copy to the Holiday Inn, with the newsman's name, c/o the Front Desk.

Nothing went as planned.

When Jason called the hotel on the agreed upon day, the newsman hadn't arrived. He would never arrive. The package with the video, addressed to go to the "Front Desk" was never received by anyone, and even after inquiring of several shifts of workers on several days, the package had not shown up, was never returned to Jason, and had apparently disappeared. All this had happened about a week earlier. Then the helicopters showed up yesterday, July 14.

And now the letter across the table.

With his friend gone, Dave left the diner without his usual coffee and hopped in his car. He drove out of the gas station, turned right, then another immediate right towards the tollbooth for the Pennsylvania Turnpike. He slowed at the toll, grabbed his ticket, then shot south towards Delaware County under the gray clouds of paranoia. Immediately, he noticed a white car with lit low-beams behind him. This was a tad odd since Dave always drove ten miles below the speed limit of 65mph. Everyone passed him. But this car stayed a short distance behind him, with the lights on despite the daytime.

What the hell has happened to Jason? Dave thought as lush Pennsylvania foothills rolled along beside him. *UFOs, helicopters, Mexican news reporter. It sounds like a Steven Spielberg movie. I know Jason doesn't drink or take drugs, so that's out. I've seen some UFOs myself. I know they're real. But still, all this government crap.* Dave pondered on as the country's first Turnpike sped beneath his wheels.

Up ahead, Dave noticed an Essex green 4x4 Jeep parked along the road. He didn't know why, but he had to keep looking at the 4x4. As he passed it, he noticed the driver was a Caucasian male, sporting a white dress shirt with an outlandishly bright, patterned tie. He sat in the most awkward, bolt-upright position with his head twisted completely to his right, away from the road. He seemed to be feigning sleep but his posture was as unnatural as it was uncomfortable.

What the hell was the matter with that *guy?* Dave thought to himself between wonderments about Jason's recent UFO adventures and the threat of government intervention.

A few more miles down the road Dave spied another car parked on the side of the highway. The closer he got to it the more unsettled he became. It was a second Essex green 4x4. "What is the likelihood of two of the same brand and color of car being parked on the turnpike," he wondered with suspicion. He slowed his car a little, feeling his curiosity pressed into overtime. As his car coasted by, there in the driver's seat was a near identical human match to the previous green car. The white male sat rigid in the seat, face turned stiffly away from the road, white shirt, weird tie.

It hit him like an H-bomb that Jason's story was real. Men from some "agency" with unmarked cars, and probably helicopters, were after Jason and now Dave. The whole thing could easily find him dead in a ditch from an "unforeseen accident." Dave's spine iced over.

"My god, I am being followed," he said so loud that he scared himself.

Unexpectedly, the white car that was following him jerked off the road like a foul ball to right field. It was clear to Dave that the driver of the white car had been listening to him somehow for a possible conversation with Jason, or anyone. This implied use of some kind of high tech spy microphone. Dave was officially paranoid.

As if to confirm suspicions of a government conspiracy, another few miles down the road found a third Essex green 4x4 with the third Caucasian man set up like a wood board in his seat, head turned hard right, with a white shirt and clown-like tie. There was no way that was coincidence: three identical cars, with three men in identical sitting positions, wearing white shirts with similar bozo-ties. The implications of Dave's experience, following on the immediate heals of Jason's nervous letter, was profound.

The American government would not send expensive helicopters to harass one UFO enthusiast, pay an agent to park outside his house all night, and have four separate cars and drivers monitoring his fellow-enthusiast without having a reason of paramount importance. UFOs were the only subject discussed between Dave and Jason that touched on national security — a security the government cannot provide when facing the enormously superior technology and thought processes of advanced alien beings. Did government agents feel that there was some strange connection to Jason and UFO sightings? Were aliens communicating with Jason and compelling him to come to them.

Jason followed the lights at the school; an alien globe followed Jason to his house; helicopters followed Jason everywhere; and agents followed Dave on the Turnpike.

It was all about the following.

After that day, Dave never again felt that he was under surveillance by unmarked cars or black helicopters. Over the years, he continued strong into the unraveling of the UFO phenomenon, seeing and learning many strange things.

He never heard from or saw Jason again.

Chapter 8.
Most Hallowed Ground
Gettysburg, Adams County

**This nation, under God, shall have
a new birth of freedom.**

~*Abraham Lincoln*
16th President, from
The Gettysburg Address

Ellen and Barry loved to visit Gettysburg for the history, ghosts, and bed-and-breakfasts. But UFOs weren't supposed to be part of the national heritage.

During July 1-3, 1863, Gettysburg, Pennsylvania became the death ground of over 50,000 people. This was the highest death toll of any Civil War battle, and included one civilian death, that of Jenny Wade, who was struck by a stray bullet that blasted through her front door and hit her in the back while she was baking bread. Gettysburg was the turning point of the war with General Lee's loss to General Meade. On the third day, the Union finally stopped the brave confederates who reached the Union line during Pickett's Charge.

Today, the huge battlefield with its numerous sub-battles, like The Wheatfield, Culp's Hill,

and The Devil's Den, is dotted with hundreds of monuments to humanity's greatest folly.

Ellen and Barry spent days studying the maps, following battle movements and reading plaques under statues. When days were done they hopped on the Farnsworth House Ghost Tours and saw ghosts every time. There had been stories about seeing orbs out on the battlefield at night, particularly on the field where Pickett's Charge had occurred.

Ellen had an idea.

"Barry, why don't we go out to the High Water Mark area to see if any ghosts or orbs are there?" she asked, giving Barry a cute smile to help entice him out of his after-dinner-with-big-dessert stupor.

"Honey, people aren't allowed in the park at night. You know that."

She knew he was hoping that his statement would puncture her adventure balloon and get him to his favorite Monday night TV show courtesy of Super 8.

"We're not permitted to walk around in the park after dark, true. But we can drive through the Pickett's Charge area on Emmitsburg Road. Maybe we'll see something."

"C'mon, you saw some ghost orbs on the tour tonight. Don't push your luck."

"But I want to see more," she whined to accent her adamancy. "The lady at the restaurant during dinner was telling her son about a full-body ghost she saw walking in the field. Just a quick ride up and down the road. That's all." Ellen put on her coat and Barry knew they were leaving.

Emmitsburg Road cut southeast through the National Park and was accessible from any area of Gettysburg. Once past the restaurants, museums, and souvenir traps, the southern Pennsylvania night dives into a blackness that is extra deep over the slaughter ground that was the Battle of Gettysburg. There are few streetlights beyond the park. But the few that exist help little to wash out the dark void, or lower the feeling of terror and horror that hangs in the air 150 years later. The two tourists kept to the low speed limit as their Dodge Neon crawled past marker after marker. Barry drove as Ellen scanned through wire-rim glasses for signs of the afterlife. Both of them expected to see a ghost or three.

Neither of them expected what happened next.

They had gone a half mile or so beyond the park boundary. There are still 200- to 300-yard-wide fields on the right heading out of town. At the far edge of the fields were thickets of trees running parallel to the road. Every few hundred yards, the trees broke for a clearing.

At the first clearing, Ellen and Barry saw two globes. One globe was on the near side of the clearing only a few feet off the ground. The other was on the far side, approximately fifteen to twenty feet up, bobbing in front of a large evergreen.

"Oh my god," Ellen exclaimed. "Look, Barry, two ghosts!"

Barry glanced back and forth between road and globes. He'd seen ghost globes and he'd seen UFO globes. The last couple days had been filled with ghost talk from Ellen, tour guides, and nervous travelers staying in haunted bed and breakfasts. So when Ellen yelled to look at the ghosts, he expected to see the soft ethereal blue-white glow of a semi-transparent light. The spirit orbs he'd seen at Gettysburg didn't radiate light, like a flashlight or lamplight.

Plus, orbs often moved in a determined direction—they seemed to be going somewhere. Too, they didn't stay visible for more than a few seconds.

UFO globes, like the ones Ellen and Barry were watching, were different. They stayed in one general area for long periods—up to a couple hours. Their light was more electric in appearance and resembled outdoor lighting that you might see at anyone's house or commercial building. Clearly, they were never attached to anything: no building, no fixture, no lamppost. And their light, which was quite bright at times, radiated a short distance in all directions.

"That's no damn ghost, El. Those lights are alien."

"What? Are you sure?" Ellen was disturbed by this announcement. "I'd just gotten used to the idea that there were such things as ghosts. Now aliens? What's next? Superman and Wonder Woman? It can't be aliens. This is Gettysburg! They can only have ghosts here."

Barry pulled the car to the side of the road for a better look at the two globes.

"Objection noted. But I'm telling you, those are alien globes. I've seen them before." Barry went into a full description of his experiences seeing these same type of devices in other parts of Pennsylvania.

Ellen felt convinced. They watched the globes for another fifteen minutes. The globes made their slight weave and bob movements, like they were studying large maps set on the ground, or hung in the trees.

"All right," said Barry, "let's go down Emmitsburg Road a little further. Maybe we'll see more globes, or maybe a ship."

"What? Are you kidding me?" Ellen was bubbling over her new experience. She felt a type of freedom; a freedom from "not knowing," from second-guessing, a freedom from experts who say "there are no such things" when she herself saw them. She liked her new freedom and the independence it implied. And she was in the perfect spot for it: Pennsylvania, the State of Independence.

"Yes, I'm kidding," Barry said with a touch of regret, seeing his friend was ready to take off with Buck Rogers.

Barry powered his Dodge Neon several more miles into the night, but they saw nothing. He left-turned into a motel driveway, retreated, then coasted back towards Gettysburg.

"Don't go too fast," Ellen snapped, as her eyes searched landscape on the right through the blackened night.

"I don't think 25 mph constitutes too fast." Barry backed off to twenty.

There were no signs of anything alien for the next couple of miles. As they approached the area of the first sighting, the couple could see the two globes bouncing around on the left.

"Look! Look at this!" Ellen exclaimed, hitting the window button, dropping the glass out of her way. On the right, near a lonely private home, were two more globes. Once again, one was sniffing around near the ground; the other was poking in and out of evergreen branches about twenty feet in the air. Barry zipped to the side of the road and halted the Dodge.

"I don't believe it. That's four of them all in the same general area."

"They are so strange," Ellen mused as the metallic balls of light slid unsteadily, as if trying to balance on ice.

"Do you want to walk down their driveway and get closer?" Barry asked with half sincerity. He'd always wanted to have hands-on with an alien device, but had been too timid. Now he had backup—a girlfriend to impress.

"Are you crazy?" came the feminine reply. "I'm not moving. I can see well enough from here, thank you."

The couple spent another twenty minutes observing the globes from another planet before heading back to their hotel.

"Lincoln called this area our 'most hallowed ground' in his Gettysburg Address," Barry said half to himself.

"Because America sacrificed so many people here, Northern and Southern." Ellen filled in the blank.

"I wonder if the aliens can tap into that energy?" Barry asked.

"Don't know. I only know that, *now I know*. I'm free from 'belief' and into knowing about UFOs."

For a good map of the Gettysburg battlefield go to:
http://www.gettysburg.stonesentinels.com/Tours/MainTourMenu.php

Emmitsburg Road, Route 15, Gettysburg, where first
two globes were sighted, one on either side of clearing.
This area is on the right when driving out of town.

Emmitsburg Road where second set of globes were seen bobbing near the evergreen at center. However, there were more trees in this copse, and, they were in full foliage at time of incident.

Chapter 9.
Drones
Fayetteville, Franklin County

Gerard J. Medvec

**The universe seems neither
benign nor hostile, merely indifferent.**
~*Carl Sagan*
Astronomer

It was winter. I was in the Chinquapin Hill campsite of Caledonia State Park in Fayetteville, site #103, directly across a lightly wooded area from the restroom. It had been cold all day. My hike felt good, but my shower in the poorly heated bathroom was uncomfortable. I pined for some cooked Spam and a fire fueling on wood pilfered from nearby empty campsites. I sat near the fire ring and kicked dirt and stones around the ring's bottom edge to keep the blaze from leaking out. Across a thirty-yard span of sparse woods were the well-lit restrooms. All looked the norm until I noticed one light that was out of place. This light was not on the building, but set just a few feet from the restroom near one of the older trees. It bobbed, swayed…

It was an alien globe.

It was free floating two to three feet off the ground. It bounced gently to and fro, all the while working hard at studying—the dirt? Who knows? The globe was basketball size, emitting light in every direction. But it was brighter on the area facing down. And, again, if this one was like the others previously seen, it could move that brightest spot to focus in any direction. This seemed to indicate that it was "looking," and therefore, intelligent.

Entranced by other-worldly junk studying our planet, I barely noticed a truck pull up to the bathroom. It parked in a space next to the building and only about fifteen-feet from the ball of light. The truck was facing my direction; its headlights were as two white eyes in the night.

Uh, oh, I thought. *Can the driver see the alien globe? What will he do?*

For a few moments there was no reaction. Suddenly, the passenger's door zipped open and a woman got out and ran to the bathroom like she was being chased by a Martian. After some appropriate bathroom time, she went running back, dove in through the already opened truck door, and then slammed it shut. But this time I saw her quick-glance at the globe as she passed it.

Oh, yeah. They know it's there, I thought. In my heart I was cheering for the lady. It took courage to run that close to an alien device. It could have laser-beamed her, or had her sucked up into the mother ship, or bopped her on the nose. Then again, nature is a strong motivator.

As the woman had shot back to the truck, I noticed that the globe bounced in a startled way, then moved closer to my neck of the woods by a few feet. That could be good, could be bad. It felt bad. Moving myself from the log near the dying fire to the front seat of my minivan, my battle wagon, seemed apropos. So what if my tent was brand new; it wasn't made of metal.

I kept watching the alien probe work. With the truck's passenger safely on board, I expected them to pull off and head back to wherever they were staying. It was closing on 9 p.m. The night was getting colder. But the truck held its position, perhaps with the engine running.

All was calm. The globe went back to its homework of surveying the ground.

Suddenly, the truck's passenger door swung open again and the woman, with something in hand, charged out. She got within, I'd say, ten feet of the globe, jolted her hand up in a near salute, and flashed off a camera shot. Back to the truck she fled.

Wow. That was brave, smart, and simply awesome. Now she had a souvenir photo of her visit to Caledonia State Park, showing one of its natural, wild, alien probes. For this bravado I punched my car horn for three short blasts. I wanted the humans to know I loved what they did and I was on their side. No signal came back from the truck, its white eyes blank.

During its photo shoot, the globe made no noticeable changes in attitude, not even a pose. It continued to analyze the same small spot on our planet that it had been studying for the last hour.

I really wanted some form of rise from the truck people just to feel that they loved me. I flashed my headlights a couple times to assure that I could see them, that I knew they had taken that picture, and that they had my blessing. Still no answer from the humans. They were as alien to me as everything else near that restroom.

The globe had been floating the whole time just slightly left of directly in front of me. My eyes had been riveted to it and the truck drama for over an hour. My head then twisted to the right a bit to relieve a kink.

And that's when I saw them.

Two, almost black, straight, metallic pipes with gently pointed ends, were hanging down from something in or above the trees. The pipes were hollow and resembled dual-exhausts from a sports car. They were two-three inches in diameter, about fifteen-feet off the ground, about one to two-feet apart. The pipes had to be connected somewhere up higher, because they moved in unison. But from my chicken's roost in the van, I couldn't see the rest of the machine. This machine moved in a slow, erratic, just-like-the-globes pattern through the evergreens on my right to farther right and eventually out of sight without disturbing the trees. This took about twenty minutes. Several times, both pipes emitted wisps of smoke at the same time. And while that implies internal combustion, there was no sound of pistons pumping, no sound at all. The smoke only exhausted three times.

Like with all the sightings I've had, I thought about getting out of the van and walking up to the pipes. I had never seen anything like them. It would have been an educational opportunity. It could also have been nuts. Maybe someday when I have backup, I'll go for it — but only with a four-inch diameter chain around my chest and waist with the other end anchored to a nuclear warhead.

Finally, the pipes drifted far enough to the right that they disappeared into the evergreens. The truck people didn't attempt any snapshots of the pipes. Probably, they didn't see them. If the pipes ever saw us, there was no indication. Neither the pipes nor the globe seemed to care that we were around. They were dedicated employees of the firm.

This whole time the globe kept at its task, never wavered, never left the general area near the trees. Maybe these are the real reasons people are afraid of the woods. It's not about the discomfort of having no laundry down the hall, or no euro mattress topper. It might be the stories their acquaintances brought home from a weekend at the park, and how they saw far-out alien stuff. Or they could have been firsthand witnesses to something they couldn't explain, something that ripped the common sense right off of their backs. And they vowed never to return.

It scared me even though the devices gave me no reason to fear. I slept in the van that night snuggled in my sleeping blanket, ready to hit the ignition if anything odd got too close. Nothing did. The two devices of that night bored their way into my memory as tools of their regime, doing what they were designed to do, and indifferent to the antics of the unfriendly monkeys taking pictures and flashing car lights.

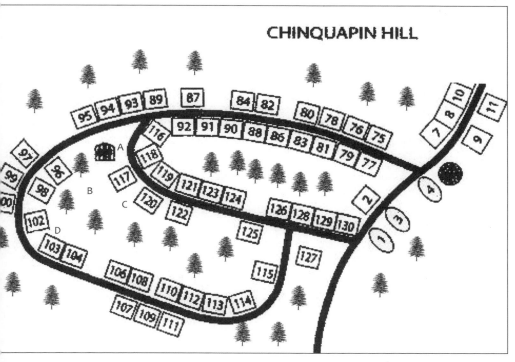

Chinquapin Hill campgrounds in Caledonia State Park.
A= restroom where alien probe and campers collide; **B**= approximate probe location; **C**= approximate location of "pipes;" **D**= Medvec's campsite #103. Artist's rendering.

Chapter 10

Peter's Principle
Loyalsock, Lycoming County

**Had the price of looking
been blindness, I would have looked.**
~Ralph Ellison
Novelist, literary critic, and scholar

The first UFO experience for Peter was when he was nine years old. It was an October Friday evening in 1985, around 9:30. His mom had just surprised him after dinner with a brand new Bushnell telescope, and Peter had assembled this first real piece of scientific equipment at a happy-new-owner's pace. He eagerly cleaned the lenses with alcohol as a finishing touch. That night was to be about stargazing.

But with the first glances from his first scope, Peter saw more than what the astronomy textbooks predicted.

Peter was in his bedroom on Shiffler Avenue, a lane lined with single homes in Loyalsock, Pennsylvania. The town is slightly northeast of its big brother, Williamsport, the county seat of Lycoming County, an area, for some reason, abuzz with aliens.

Known as the Lumber Capital during the 1800s, Williamsport was producing over 340 million board feet per day, the highest production of lumber in the world. Consequently, the logging industry in north central Pennsylvania made many millionaires. And when people make millions, they spend millions, a lot of it on their homes. This was universally the case in nineteenth century Williamsport. Today, the Historical Preservation Society of Williamsport strives to maintain the architectural excellence that exists along the "Millionaires Row" of homes.

The nearby towns of Loyalsock, Montoursville, Pennsdale, and Hughesville, all part of the Williamsport Metro area, ensure the feeling of small town, rural mountain Pennsylvania.

And a dark, rural mountain zone makes for better UFO watching.

Peter pointed the telescope out the window for his first close look at the moon. It was grand in its new detail: The Sea of Tranquility in the northeast, the Ocean of Storms in the far southwest, the Tyco crater due south. It was breathtaking. Yet, for a moment, Peter felt a bit guilty. A foreign planet was suddenly bigger than life, brightly discernible. He felt as if he was glimpsing something meant only for older eyes. He jerked his head up from the scope.

"If only Mom could see this," he thought out loud. His mother was blind and would never know the serenity of a Pennsylvania autumn day, let alone the surface features of a distant world. But she was Peter's biggest fan.

Peter stared at the moon. All was well. The lunar neighbor sat pensively against the massive backdrop of the Universe. And that's what bothered him. It was his mother's "older eyes" that should be seeing these wonders, not just his. All the same, he thought a look around other parts of the heavens, with the new gift his mother gave him, was a good plan. That way he could give his mother a gift in return: a livelier, fuller description of the night sky. He would electrify her imagination, showing her inner eyes the cosmos through his outer ones. Peter set his head against the eyepiece on the telescope and shifted his view to another part of the night heavens.

Something froze his hand on the knob.

There, among all the usual stars, was one light that didn't fit. It was five to six times bigger than the surrounding points of light. He looked up from the eyepiece, could barely see the odd ball of light, then gazed through the Bushnell again. Then he focused the scope on the object, turning the rack and pinion focusing knob with his left hand and twisting the eyepiece with his right as fast as he could. The object came into clarity, and was now stranger looking than ever.

When gazing at celestial bodies through a telescope, there is little doubt about what you are seeing, usually. The moon is solid, other planets are solid; you cannot see through them. This big light, however, was perfectly round and had black wavy lines going through it that gave it a semi-transparent appearance. Some of that, admittedly, may have been Peter's inexperience with the telescope. There were quite a few knobs to adjust. The object also had a wild collection of flashing lights in stationary orbit around its edge. The lights were not attached to the large center globe, but were more like a perfectly suspended string of white Christmas lights without the wires.

Peter had lived near the Williamsport Regional Airport his whole life. Even at nine years old, he knew what planes looked like, how helicopters flew, and what type of FAA lights they all had to have. This object had none of that. Ninety-five percent of the time planes at the local airport took off and landed east to west, due to the prevailing wind. The large, round light with its halo of smaller lights was not moving. It was uncharacteristic with anything that Peter had seen before. It stood out. Way out.

Something occurred to him and he tore his head away from the scope.

What if they can see me looking at them... he thought. His mind began a review of science fiction scenarios he'd enjoyed on TV and in the movies. *Maybe they'd blow up our whole town*, he quivered at the idea. *Or*, the last part of the thought was hard coming, *they could shoot a laser through the telescope right into my eye.* The boy's concept of being sightless took on a new meaning. *How would I help Mom?* Peter considered his mother's everyday struggles. He compared her to the moms of his playmates with all their vision intact. And while his mom was a little different, that was all there was — a little difference. She was much like all the other moms, only better. *I wonder what Mom would do if she were me,* his young mind inquired, as he looked towards the odd light amongst the stars.

Peter looked again through the telescope and watched the object for another ten minutes. Then he ran downstairs to the living room to tell his mom.

"Mom, come to my room. Quick! I've been watching this big ball in the sky." His excitement was catching like an airborne flu.

"Really," she answered with mounting enthusiasm as she got up from her chair.

"Hurry up!" Peter had already spun around and was flying back up the steps to his room.

"All right, all right. I'm right behind you," she called, as she dropped her braille novel and paced herself through every step and turn she needed to get up to her son's room.

Peter was fighting frantically with the telescope as his mom slid herself onto the side of his bed.

"Tell me every little detail, Peter."

At first, there was silence.

"Peter, what do you see?"

"It's gone."

"Are you sure? Did the telescope move? Or could the ball have moved somewhere else in the sky?"

"I guess. But I don't see it any-where, Mom." Peter's disappoint-ment leaked into his mother's ears.

"How long did you watch it?"

"Oh, about ten minutes."

"That's wonderful, honey," she said, as she crossed the room and instinctively put a hand on his shoulder, without a thought, without a miss. "Maybe it was a UFO."

"I think so." Peter's face re-mained attached to the Bushnell's eyepiece, moving the scope up and down, left and right, trying to recapture the vision of other-worldliness so he could give his mother the full benefit of a first-hand account.

But it was gone.

They were quiet for a minute.

"Chin up, honey," his mother said, as she started out of the room, wanting to make it all better, and, perhaps, feeling a bit clairvoy-ant, "You'll see something again. Trust me."

Moms are always right.

The Philosophy of V
Montoursville, Lycoming County

Philosophy will always show, that a vast, perhaps the larger portion of the truth arises from the seemingly irrelevant.
~Edgar Allen Poe
Author, poet, editor

Driving across the Broad Street Bridge over Loyalsock Creek in Montoursville, Pennsylvania, Pe-ter and Mike saw seven lights in the sky shaped like a perfect "v," or arrow's head. Peter's mother had been right. It was his second sighting. But unlike the first event, being older and more wary of the world, his nerves began to rattle like marbles in a tin cup.

It was a fresh summer night in August 1993, under a dark blue sky. Peter, now seventeen, was driving his friend Mike home to their town of Loyalsock. They had just finished an entire aisle-by-aisle, rack-by-rack inspection of the new Walmart that opened on N. Loyalsock Avenue, in Mon-toursville. It was the small town thing to do. The time was around 8:30 p.m. The V was flying north-ward, following Loyalsock Creek, perpendicular to the bridge. They were only a half mile away from the Williamsport Airport, south of the bridge. The lights on the craft were extremely bright, but they did not beam downwards like spotlights. It was one solid craft.

"What is that?" Peter sput-tered as his head metronomed back and forth between the road and the V.

"We've never seen anything like it," Mike noted, referring to both boys' extensive study of fly-ing machines.

"Might be Air Force," Peter suggested.

Peter and Mike tentatively planned to join the Air Force after high school. They had studied every military and commercial aircraft so they could identify them on sight. Each of them could spit out the differences between an F15 and an F16 on a sergeant's command. They knew flying machines.

"The shape of the craft looks like an exaggerated cross between a B2 Bomber and F-117 Stealth Bomber. But more like a perfect arrowhead," Peter clarified.

Just off the bridge they turned right onto Warrenville Road to follow the V northward. Doing 50mph, they were able to keep up with the spaceship. Mike leaned out the passenger window.

"There's no sound. How can that be?" He fell back into his seat, and looked worried.

"This thing is huge. It should be loud as hell." Peter tried hard to gel all the information he was getting with his senses with the book info he had in his head. There was no match.

He snapped the steering wheel to the right to keep his car on the road.

"Seems like only about 1,000 feet up," said Mike.

"Well, that's illegal. It may be under the radar even though we're less than a mile from the airport," Peter replied. "Plus it's flying north. No one ever flies north. Everything flies east and west. There's nothing up north except trees."

"The wingspan must be at least 300 feet!" Mike exclaimed, as he continued studying the large, silent V in the sky.

"And it's only doing about 50mph and I can't see any engines or propellers. What's holding it up?" Peter wondered.

"Exactly. Go faster. It's getting lost in the trees."

But faster did not help. Warrensville Road continued its sweep alongside Loyalsock Creek. Lined on the right with large evergreens and maples, every skyward glance was blocked.

The machine was gone.

Peter turned left onto 4 Mile Drive to take Mike back to Loyalsock. They talked excitedly about the V until they pulled in front of his house. This was nothing like anything they had ever seen before. What could this possibly be?

"If I see it again on my way home, I'll call you," Peter assured Mike.

"You better," his friend said with a chuckle, his face still lit with signs of the thrill.

Peter started off towards his own home on Shiffler Road. It only took a few minutes for him to see the V again. This time it was over the west end of Williamsport, about five and a half miles southwest of where he and Mike first saw it, now roughly 2,000 feet up, too far for him to chase. Besides, the distance did not matter. A moment later it simply vanished.

Peter sped home and called Mike as promised. They chattered on about how the V was completely out of the ordinary. No FAA strobe lights were anywhere on the machine. Plus the seven large, white lights that were on it were illegal, as far as the FAA would have been concerned. There were no Air Force bases near Williamsport, Pennsylvania, so the likelihood of an amazing experimental craft being test flown over the 115,000+ residents of Lycoming County was ridiculous. In addition, it was flying too low.

Peter states his philosophy best.

It was amazing! Thinking about it today, however, it's pitiful that YouTube and the Internet put so many made-up videos, possibly for attention, possibly for some other reason, into the public's hands. The fake videos diminish the truth of what people actually see. It discredits the real UFO sighting. Because so much fakery has been done with the UFO phenomenon, when the subject comes up, and you tell people what you have truly seen, they tend to brush you off as just another attention seeker trying to upstage the conversation. When something so out of the norm hits you, it leaves a lasting dent in your psyche. Looking back, the event makes me feel an inch high. Obviously, other things are going on in this world. And when you become part of it, what do you do? Maybe you write a book. Maybe you sit on the information because you don't want to be ridiculed. It's sad because you cannot have a sensible conversation with most people about the event.

However, there is no discrediting it for Peter. He knows what he saw. Period. He still lives near the Williamsport Airport. He still sees planes and helicopters every day. But that V will always be part of the larger truth.

Twenty-Five Minutes
Hughesville, Lycoming County

The only thing that interferes with my learning is my education.
~Albert Einstein
Physicist

Nothing warms up a cold November morning in northern Pennsylvania like a shot of hot java, a shot of driving-to-work reality, and a shot of something silver unexplainably skipping across the 7 a.m. sky. That morning, in 2011, would super-heat Peter's insides for a long time.

Peter worked for a natural gas and oil company, maintaining pipes, valves, and stations in good repair across Pennsylvania. The job site for that day's work was only about twenty-five minutes from his house in Pennsdale. Peter was following his co-worker and buddy, Rob, who was in a truck in front of him, driving east on Route 220 to Hughesville. It was a nice, clear morning. Peter was in his own truck, Wawa coffee in hand, headed for another day of hard work in the woodlands.

As they rolled up to the only stop sign in Hughesville, Peter saw a white, silver streak go from south to north across the entire sky in a couple of seconds.

It actually skipped across the sky, but seemed to appear and disappear as it went, like a blinking light moving fast. When he could see the object; it looked either silver or like a white light. It was visible more than it was not, and appeared to make dash marks in the sky as it flew. It had started out only about a quarter mile ahead of their position and about a thousand feet up. It was a small object. It traveled at a slight incline. The speed of the item was so fast it blurred any real shape the object might have displayed.

At first, Peter thought it was a reflection on his windshield. But he knew it wasn't. He snapped the CB radio from the dashboard and called Rob in the truck ahead of him.

"Did you see that?" Peter asked without any identification of what "that" could have been. An honest answer was all he wanted from his friend, and he was careful not to lead Rob's thinking process.

"Yeah, Pete. What the hell was that streak across the sky? Do you think it was a meteorite or something? That was really weird."

"Couldn't be a meteorite. It was headed upward," Peter answered, maybe a bit too relaxed. This was not his first lap around the UFO track.

"Yeah, you're right. Amazing." The CB clicked off.

The two men talked for about ten minutes about the happening after they reached the job sight.

Peter loved this sighting because his work buddy saw the item, too. And he saw it from a different angle than Peter so there was no chance it could be a reflection bouncing off both windshields when two different angles were involved.

In his entire lifetime, Peter had experienced only about twenty-five minutes of UFO phenomena. What he learned in that short time is more meaningful than any college degree, any religious sermon, or any company training program. He learned how to be big enough to admit he was small. Those twenty-five minutes kept Peter sharp, always searching, realistic. Those twenty-five minutes, out of thirty-five years, has earned him a master's degree, at least.

Chapter 11.
The Air Show
Newberry, Lycoming County

**The soul should always stand ajar,
ready to welcome the ecstatic experience.**
~Emily Dickinson
19th century poet

Seven lights were dancing in the sky. They reclassified the content of the conversation on the front porch from fringe to prophetic.

Sabrina, husband Peter, and daughter Marnie, rented the first floor apartment in a house on Clark Street in Newberry, Pennsylvania, just west of the Newberry Town Park. It was a clear and beautiful June night in 2011. Sabrina and Marnie, her landlord Gary, her upstairs neighbors Jeanette and Tyrone and their three kids, and Bev, the local skeptic from across the alley, were all outside talking on Sabrina's front porch as they often did. It was fun to hang out with the locals and solve the problems of the world. The time was about 9:45 p.m. That night, one problem would not be fixed with a few finger-points and strong words.

Gary was Newberry's UFO expert. His property was a spacious one up the street with a large backyard butted up against forest. Positioned in his backyard, around the clock, were several weather-proof cameras, both video and still. These were rigged with motion sensors and aimed at the sky to catch the flyby of anything normal or extraterrestrial.

Sabrina was always amused by Gary's stories. He was constantly retelling news reports and articles that he had read about the latest UFO happenings. She had heard him tell many times about the various supposedly alien crafts he had caught on film with his own cameras. He was Mr. UFO. On first meeting with strangers, Sabrina often felt he could easily have been misconstrued as a nut job.

But Sabrina was about to find out once and for all that he was not.

"Since Marnie likes to video stuff," Gary was, yet again, telling Sabrina, "let her set up a tripod in your yard and record things in the sky. Maybe she'll catch a UFO. You know I have."

"All that equipment is expensive, Gary. I was lucky I could buy her a little camera," Sabrina reminded her landlord.

To gently press his point, Gary looked at the sky and began describing a UFO that he had once seen. "I'll never forget the time I filmed that torpedo-shaped—"

"Gary, if I was meant to see a UFO," Sabrina interrupted what was at least the fifth time he had told that story, as she looked and lightly waved her right hand upward, "then I would see..." Her voice trailed off weakly and her mouth froze in the open position.

The other adults looked at her, then followed her gaze to the sky. There, bouncing around as if in between pinball bumpers, was a ball of light. As all eyes focused upon it, the light stopped moving and hovered, seeming to study the humans who were studying it. Or, perhaps, it was just saying hello. The ball was 1,200 to 1,500 feet up and of indeterminate size.

"That's just some kind of airplane," Tyrone said as if he was trying to convince himself, and for an instant this was the common

consensus as second guessing got underway. But the ball did not move.

"People, that can't be a plane," Gary noted. "It's not moving. It's another UFO! See, I told you to look up."

"Wow," Bev the skeptic exclaimed in an unusual, non-skeptical way, "I've never seen anything like that!"

"That'a girl, Bev, keep an open mind," Gary taunted.

"I've been to several air shows and seen all kinds of crazy flying machines," Sabrina started, "but there has never been anything like that. This is not an air show item. It's just sitting there." She had barely finished the sentence when the ball of light began shifting from side to side. It did that for a couple of seconds, after which it shot straight up and disappeared somewhere above the atmosphere. The small audience applauded.

Bev ran home and got her camera/phone so she could film the object if it returned. Sabrina popped into her apartment for her own cassette video recorder. Everyone talked excitedly about the strange lighted object. The kids were running around acting out sci-fi scenes they remembered from the movies and Saturday night TV. Gary was boasting about how prevalent aliens were, and how they would show up almost on demand. All eyes were trained upwards.

The glowing object suddenly appeared in view. It performed a repeat of the earlier display. But this time, six other lighted globes, smaller than the original, accompanied it. When they were not darting around the sky in a haphazard pattern, they hovered close to the larger device. Sabrina could hear a slight humming sound while the aerial show progressed. The sound ceased, however, whenever the crafts all came to a stop in the air. Upon moving again, the hum returned. When they left, they all bolted together straight up towards space and were gone.

"Oh my god, they are so maneuverable," Sabrina exclaimed.

"Did you get pictures, Mommy?" her daughter Marnie asked.

"Got them right here, dear."

The next few minutes traversed in silence, as the noisy neighbors had subsided into hopeful observers, waiting for the next display of out-worlder entertainment. But the performance was over.

"Let's watch it again," Sabrina announced as she began to rewind her cassette recorder. But as she did, it began to make a grinding noise. "What the heck is with this?" She fiddled with the buttons, got no result, and forced open the door to the cassette. The tape from the cassette spilled out of the camera with creases and damage that made it un-viewable and un-rewindable. The treasured images they believed were caught on video were gone.

"Hey, my phone's not working either," Bev whined with agitation. She pounded the phone into her palm angrily but got no response from it. Strangely, the camcorder and the cell phone stopped working at the same time. No coincidence.

Later, Bev was able to get her phone working. When she played the UFO video back, however, the entire recording showed up as only an illuminated red screen, as if someone had pointed a red laser beam directly into the lens during the entire recording. No UFO images were visible.

The entire UFO show lasted about fifteen minutes. There was nothing top-secret about it. Sabrina knew it was not a plane, not one of the famous and prolific "'weather balloons" that the government kept insisting that everyone was seeing. The group of neighbors had maintained open hearts and minds. Because so many people saw them, and everyone said they saw them, that took away any chance that Sabrina's imagination had created illusions in her mind.

It was the best of the air shows.

Chapter 12.
A Few Very Short Stories

A collection of short descriptions of sightings—courtesy of International UFO Museum and Research Center, Roswell, New Mexico; The National UFO Reporting Center (www.ufocenter.com); and Filer's Files.com.

Bellefonte, Center County
September 30, 2005; approximately 10:30 a.m.

A witness saw a flying tubular-shaped object that looked like a black, telephone pole in length and size. It flew across the Penn State campus near the airport towards Philadelphia. There were several low-flying planes close to the object. Other witnesses arrived and several reported the object to 911. The airport was also called, and while they confirmed that something was in the air, they said there was no need for concern.

Breezewood, Bedford County
May 27, 2007; approximately 11:30 p.m.

The clouds were a light haze with the stars dimly shining through, when the witness saw a bright light suddenly appear directly above him. The light grew brighter until it was as bright as the moon. It then lost its glow and moved slowly northwest, passing one of the stars still visible through the haze. After twenty minutes, a green light appeared heading north. This object slowly pulsated between dim and bright and had a blue tint at its brightest.

Carlisle, Cumberland County
April 2, 2003; approximately 9:45 p.m.

A flying triangle with a light in each corner was seen about six miles outside of Carlisle. The witness was star gazing towards the Big Dipper at a small cluster of shooting stars, when to his amazement the black triangle suddenly appeared over his head, and was much too low to be an aircraft. It silently glided south across the sky for thirty seconds.

Gettysburg, Adams County
June 1, 2002; approximately 10 p.m.

Two students were lying on a blanket on the Gettysburg Battlefield up the hill from the college, when they noticed lights or stars moving around the sky past a tall lookout tower. They first traveled in a straight line, then would stop, and then accelerate forward three times in short bursts. The lights then made a zigzag pattern at incredible speeds before vanishing.

Hanover, York County
March 23, 1974; approximately 12:55 a.m.

Two officers for the Pennsylvania Game Commission were on patrol when they suddenly spotted a glowing cigar-shaped object about 300 yards from their vehicle. The object looked like a giant fuselage about six times longer than their car. It was silent, but emitted a pulsating light towards the ground.

Hershey, Dauphin County
February 2, 2006; approximately 6 p.m.

Four horizontal orange lights were observed in the sky by one witness. Then one by one the lights went out. The lights reappeared showing the object flying vertically. It then switched to diagonally. One single orange light went on and off twice. A few moments later, the area was flown over by F-16 fighter jets.

Hollidaysburg, Blair County
July 14, 1998; approximately 10 p.m.

A witness driving on Route 22 saw three blue-white triangular lights that formed an inverted "V" flying overhead. The object hovered motionless for about forty-five seconds, then suddenly "exploded" and disappeared from sight.

Mechanicsburg, Cumberland County
September 4, 2007; approximately 10 p.m.

From his bedroom, a witness saw a star-like object change colors from red to white. The light moved slightly to the right, then back, then slightly up, and then back again. Through binoculars, the object was plate-like with blinking lights in a straight line around the edge of the saucer. The lights changed colors from red to ivory to green to white. The object remained stationary for about an hour, then faded away from the viewer.

Red Lion, York County
August 30, 2011; approximately 10:40 a.m.

From her balcony, a witness saw a large symmetrical disc fly between two radio towers. Familiar with many types of aircraft, the witness realized this craft lacked definition. While trying to photograph it, the object gathered speed, moved several miles out over the Susquehanna River, then pitched up into some clouds and was gone.

Spring Grove, York County
December 27, 2009; approximately 5:45 a.m.

The witness glanced out the bedroom window and saw a bright red light in the sky. Opening the window, he heard a low hum. The object was just above the tree tops about fifty yards away. Three landing legs were hanging down, and were covered in red, green, blue, and amber lights. The witness flicked his outside lights on and off, and the white light underneath the flying object changed to a blue-green color. The object appeared square shaped with lights at each corner and a light in the middle. From that middle light, a beam was shot downward, but it didn't reach the ground.

State College, Centre County September 18, 2010; approximately 10 p.m.

From outside their camper, after a Penn State football game, witnesses saw an orange-yellow flame, smaller at the front than at the rear, soaring noiselessly over the campground at a low altitude. It then turned to the right at a sharp angle and started to gain altitude and speed. It took several minutes for it to disappear.

Williamsport, Lycoming County May 1, 2011; approximately 5 a.m.

That Sunday morning, while driving, the witness noticed a red ball of light in the sky. About fifty feet away from the red ball was a circle or saucer-like object with four different colored lights underneath: yellow, green, blue, and red. The objects disappeared over the mountains.

York, York County March 9, 2009; approximately 10:20 p.m.

Two witnesses watched a blinding bright, octagon-shaped UFO approach. It was the size of a 747 aircraft with half the wing size added on each side. There were six large yellow lights with two smaller ones next to each of the six large ones. The largest lights were on the outer edge.

Chapter 13.
The Uninvited
Harrisburg, Dauphin County

**Courage is resistance to fear,
mastery of fear, not absence of fear.**

~Mark Twain

WHO IS IN MY ROOM? Suzy shouted from her mind, since the words could not pass her lips. She was paralyzed.

It was a cool autumn Saturday morning in 1979 as dawn split the horizon over the suburbs of the state capital of Pennsylvania: Harrisburg. Purplish hues gave way to lighter shades of blue as splashes of amber dashed through the windows and hallways of the house where ten-year-old Suzy lived.

Suzy had been asleep until an unearthly crinkling sound at the doorway broke her from her slumber. And she found she could not move. An invisible force was holding her down on her bed. She struggled to catch her breath through a frozen, parted mouth. Her arms clung to her sides as if glued, but her fingers, the only working parts of her body, strangled the blankets on her bed with a grip that would have crushed pineapples.

Ricky, is that you? she hoped to herself. There was someone in the hall, behind the wall to the right of her doorway. It was common for her younger brother, Ricky, to wander the morning floors and peek around the corner into her room through the sheer curtains that took the place of a door. He would want her to get up and play. It did not feel like Ricky.

Suddenly, she glimpsed a partial face with one large eye from the edge of the door frame. It was not Ricky.

Who is that? her mind trembled with wonder, unable to see the reality of the being's face. In that instant, the unknown person went from the hallway to inside her room at the foot of the bed. Peering over the edge of the bed frame, about four feet tall, with a bulbous head and black, almond-shaped soulless eyes, was an alien creature. It had slits for a nose and a tiny mouth, all of its body was colorless gray flesh. Suzy was trapped as just beyond her toes the eyes stared at her.

Yet Suzy had no point of reference for this vision; never before had she seen such a thing. Her strict, religious parents kept the children busy with chores and school work and away from the influence of the idiot box/boob tube/television, so her awareness of news media and science fiction was almost non-existent. Her mind said maybe this *was* her brother.

Ricky, what are you doing? she thought softly. She was certain it was him, but her mind was protecting her, either by choice or by force, from seeing the being's true features.

Then she noticed something... something that slipped past the parapet of her mental fortress. Whoever it was couldn't be Ricky, because it was too tall, and it couldn't be her older brother, Thomas, either, because it was too short.

Suzy's paralyzed body was dipped in a coating of terror. *WHO IS IN MY ROOM?* There was a stranger there. Its true appearance became clear. Suzy wanted to run, scream, cry, fight, hide. She could do none of these. Her breath came harder. Fingers pressed chewed nails deep into palms. Her arms remained pinned at her sides, though she wanted to rub her eyes in disbelief, eyes that were now locked in a staring contest with...something, some creature from another place.

Seconds passed. Though feeling drained from the being's stare, her breathing eased. Suzy watched and waited. She was bound to escape the mental clutches of her unwanted guest. Lessons learned about inner strength began to surface in her young heart. Suzy took in deeper breaths and summoned her courage through the spirit within her. She mentally pushed and pulled at her fingers, forcing them to open and close with expanding distance. She was breaking loose from paralysis. Then, with both hands, Suzy pulled herself up from the bed, sitting up straight facing her antagonist. Shivering from the lack of blood flow and fear of the intruder, she was going to order him out!

Suddenly, the being vanished before her eyes without a sound, without a trace. She was back to free movement. She owned her body again for a moment, and then, with a tsunami of fear, she panicked and screamed aloud for someone to rescue her.

Thirty-three years later, Suzy would realize that what she saw that morning in her room was a "grey," an alien type associated with abductions and other sightings. Her story was told with passion and conviction, with no doubts to its authenticity. For Suzy, this was the beginning of a lifetime of experiences that related to the supernatural and other-worldly.

Why was the being there? What was it doing? Was it using some type of telekinetic power to hold Suzy inside its grasp? Had it been there before and was this the first time that she caught its routine? These beings are vastly intelligent, yet it let itself be discovered by a ten-year-old girl. There was a design and a purpose to that visitor being there, but we will never rationalize its true intent. Was it a three-dimensional alien or an inter-dimensional traveler?

A monster visiting a child's room is nothing new. There are thousands of nearly identical circumstances reported worldwide throughout recent decades and long before. Even ancient fables may have been based on the original author's memories of a terrifying childhood visit from something other-worldly. Logical then, that children's bedtime practices often include having a courageous parent search under the bed and peer into closets for the uninvited. Not everything that raises chills in the night may come from an overactive imagination.

Chapter 14.
Student of the Stars
Lancaster, Lancaster County

And I can say that I am grateful that I got this lesson very early.
~Gunther Grass
Novelist, playwright, 1999
Nobel Prize for Literature

Louis has the gravity to pull UFOs down to his location. All the stories in this collection are about one man who, at the crux, has grown up with UFOs and related phenomena. While not an abductee (as far as he knows), an astronomer, or a MUFON (Mutual UFO Network) member, he is in a real sense a "star man."

The Man in Black

Seven-year-old Louis didn't remember how he'd gotten downstairs. His second-floor bed was comfortable enough, and he did remember going to bed and falling asleep. But somehow, between sacking out and peeling back the curtain on the back kitchen door, he had sleepwalked through the house.

And now he was screaming.

It was 1973, a nice September night, in a row home on Reynolds Avenue in the city of Lancaster. He stood at the kitchen door. Something had prompted Louis to stop at the unlocked entrance and not open the door, as he had previously felt inclined to do. His hand was on the doorknob ready to spin it to the right and pull inward. But shaking overtook his small fingers, loosening his grip. A deep inner voice reverberated inside him, telling him to release the knob. He did.

Instead, he slid the lace curtain on the door, riding on rods at top and bottom, to the left.

As he did, a horrid face stared back at him. A frightening figure was on the other side of the glass. It was a man in a black suit, wearing sunglasses in the middle of the night. Even with sunglasses on, the male face was ugly, strange, misshapen, and stern. It was definitely a man, but barely seemed human. Louis screamed again like he was being kidnapped by Beelzebub. The face in the window shifted back as the man stretched to upright. He was taller than he should have been.

Thumping was heard from upstairs and his dad's voice cracked the air like a .22 caliber. "What the hell is going on?" his dad roared. "It's 3 a.m.! What the hell are you doing outta bed and screaming like a werewolf?" He rolled into the kitchen, grasped Louis by the shoulders, and spun him around for an immediate answer.

"There's a strange man outside!" Louis cried, body shaking, falling back from the door, pointing at it like his arm was an arrow on a longbow.

"What are you doing down here?"

"I don't know."

"How do you know there's a man outside?" His dad flicked the door curtain to one side, revealing blank glass.

"There just *is*, Daddy," Louis persisted.

His dad hurried out of the kitchen, returned seconds later, opened the door, and went out carrying his shotgun. He marched into the small backyard, weapon shouldered, and scanned the interconnecting neighbors' yards for someone hopping fences during an escape, or hiding low behind a trash can. He saw no one. Quietly, he reentered the kitchen.

He pressed the door closed, twisted the lock on the doorknob, and flipped the deadbolt into place. Locking doors at night was new to him, but the hairs on his neck told him to do it. The initial agitation was over. He knew Louis must have seen something and he didn't want to upset his son any further. He laid the shotgun on the kitchen counter.

"Are you all right?" he asked, as he lifted Louis into his arms and carried him back to the safety of bed.

"I guess so," the boy shuddered as he looked over his Dad's shoulder and saw the grotesque face with sunglasses in his mind.

"It's okay now, Louis; there's no one out there. I checked everywhere. Nothing to be afraid of."

Later, as he heard his Dad downstairs locking other doors and windows, Louis tugged his blanket up around his eyes. He would never be sure if that night was one of the few true cases of sleepwalking that had occurred during his early childhood, or if he had been summoned to the kitchen by an unknown force. Without question, he is relieved he never opened that door.

A Visit to Cousin Charlie's
Millersville, Lancaster County

I am sometimes a fox and sometimes a lion. The whole secret ...lies in knowing when to be the one or the other.
~Napoleon Bonaparte
French Emperor,
early 19th Century

Louis loved visiting Cousin Charlie's house on weekends. It was a cloudy Saturday in late August 1977. Louis was eleven years old. The boys spent many of the daylight hours racing a mini-cycle with a Briggs and Stratton engine around the two-story white house — the last house in the row of single homes. Behind and to the left of his Aunt Jean's property was a large cornfield owned by the neighboring farm. Aunt Jean left the boys on their own, safe on her rural dead-end street, safe from the dangers of the modern world.

The space visitors didn't see it that way.

Louis took turns with Charlie racing circles around the house, over the driveway on the right, flying up the small hill near the back of the house on his way to the left side, churning the lawn into a muddy circus of boyhood entertainment.

On this Saturday afternoon, Louis made his last spin from right to left around the track. When he reached the hill at the back of the house, he slammed on the brakes. Up in the sky he saw three lights in a triangle formation out over the cornfield, not more than 1,000 feet in the air, partially buried in the clouds. The three different colored lights dotted the bottom tip of each corner.

"Hey, Charlie, c'mere quick," he yelled.

His cousin dashed from the front lawn to the backyard.

"Do you see that?" He pointed to the anomaly that neither boy had ever seen before — beyond a comic book or science fiction movie.

"Yeah. What the heck is that?"

As the boys watched, the lights became clearer as they fully exited the clouds, bringing the edges of a large triangular craft into full visibility.

"Whoa." Louis shut the bike off and handed the handlebar to Charlie. "I'm getting your mom," he yelled, already at the back door. "Don't let that thing out of your sight!"

Charlie stood guard at the back edge of the driveway. Aunt Jean was watching TV in bed. She was comfortable there after cooking all morning for that night's dinner. But Louis roused her with a yell, "Hey, Aunt Jean, want to see a flying saucer?"

"What?!" Moments later, she was in the backyard looking up at the oddest thing her eyes had ever beheld. Then she looked back to earth. Charlie was gone.

"Charlie. Charlie!" Both nephew and aunt hollered like their lungs needed to be rid of the name. No answer.

The triangle wasn't moving, but was hovering like a taunt above the cornfield.

"Charlie!!" Aunt Jean screeched, looking at the metallic craft, filling with desperation.

"Here I am," a small voice from hundreds of yards into the cornfield drifted to their ears. A little hand was bobbing up and down over the highest stalks. It was Charlie. He had run into the field and positioned himself directly under the UFO, refusing to let it get away.

"Charlie, you come back here this instant!" his mom hollered like she was campaigning for Mom of the Year. Charlie charged towards them, bouncing off the five-foot cornstalks, creating a shaking wake behind him.

The three were together again in the back yard. They admired the neat unearthly shape above them and its absolute silence. It was their UFO, in their neighborhood, like a gift from their god.

Then it changed.

The whole thing began to separate into three equal parts, and the mini crafts moved away equidistant to one another, at least

for a couple of seconds. After that the three craft turned away from each other and spun off at wild angles.

This roused curiosity in Louis. He wasn't scared, just enamored at the mechanical wonder of it all.

Then the crafts and their lights vanished.

Louis and his relatives walked towards the front of the house, talking excitedly about the event, thinking it was over, but knowing they were special for having seen it.

However, upon reaching the front lawn, they looked up to see, under the clouds, a large, cigar-shaped, silver fuselage without wings or tail fins, lit up underneath from tip to tip with fluorescent-style lighting in red, yellow, and green. This craft, too, was silent. A neighbor lady came out of her house across the street to join the watch.

The cigar began to move slowly to the right, and then suddenly it disappeared upward like the clear plastic cylinder put in the suction tube at the drive-in bank. It was gone. It happened so fast, there was barely time for a breath, let alone a comment.

Louis and his family entered the house, feeling worn and dazed from seeing things that their trusted government said didn't exist. That was two different sightings in less than an hour. And the day was not over.

At bedtime that night, the boys were in Charlie's bedroom on the first floor. Charlie's bed, with its headboard on an inner wall, was parallel to and out about two feet from the outer wall housing a double window with closed mini-blinds. Louis was in a sleeping bag on the floor, on the side of the bed away from the window. If anybody had looked in the window, they would not have seen him.

Hours crept by and the boys slept.

With a flash, the blinds lit up with the brightness of a small sun. Instantly awake, Louis peeked over his cousin's mattress. He knew something was wrong. His body rippled with a frightened shiver. Something was very wrong. He just knew someone was out there, even though he could barely look at the glowing mini blinds. He didn't want them to see him. It was all wrong. His skin went to arctic temperatures. He was scared out of his soul. No light should be that bright. He had to remain still so they wouldn't know he was there.

The silent blaze of unnatural light persisted for numerous terrifying minutes. Almost a pleading prayer Louis thought, *If I don't move or make a sound, I'll be safe. I'm in the sleeping bag, they can't see me.*

Intense illumination, then none. As if by a pulled plug, the light went out.

Louis jumped out of his sleeping bag and dove at the window, sliding the slippery blinds away from the glass. There was nothing to see except yard. He turned to Charlie who had sprung upright in the bed.

"Charlie, what was that light?"

"I don't know. I woke up, looked out the window, and went back to bed. I don't know why I didn't' go to my brother's room to get a better look."

"Did you look in the light?"

"I think so."

"What did you see?!"

Charlie scratched his head. "Nothing." It didn't seem like a big deal to Charlie.

The next morning, little more was said.

Over the years, Louis has had his doubts. The situation was too intense for "nothing" to have happened. He worries that his cousin may have faced more, perhaps abduction. Now thirty years have passed and Louis is *sure* more happened that night than he or Charlie can remember. For years, Louis has had a recurring dream centered on that incident. Also, other personal occurrences in recent years suggest that being terrified by lights in a window was too simplistic an act with too empty a meaning to have been embedded in his memory. Aliens have an agenda. It's bigger than we can imagine, and more cleverly executed than we could ever trace. So, while ignorance of their actions is just that, something else must be going on.

Louis thought about hypnotic regression for himself and Charlie, but never pursued it. Maybe wondering about the answer was more comforting than knowing it. Once you know it, it changes things. Your world, your mind, people around you—it all changes. In the end, Louis was content knowing the surface facts: cool UFOs, bright lights, no one got hurt.

Sock and Buskin
Lancaster, Lancaster County

Astronomy compels the soul to look upwards and leads us from this world to another.
~Plato
Philosopher,
5th Century BCE

One July in the early 1990s, Louis was outside his Lehigh Avenue house across from McKenzie High School in Lancaster city. He was married now and was performing a traditional lord-of-the-realm survey of his estate; translation—he was walking around the outside of the house looking at stuff. The roof line at the back of the house was under inspection when two delta-shaped, black wings with no running lights, and classic boomerang shapes, flew silently overhead. There was no variation in their trajectory, that is, they were not affected by wind or turbulence. They did not sway side to side, but as two stretched Vs, gliding through the sky. Louis guesstimated the wings were about twenty feet wide. He had already observed various UFOs in his life. This sighting thrilled him, as they all did, but he wasn't ready to jump out of his space suit over it.

Then he had an idea. The deltas were headed directly over his friend Tim's house a couple miles away. Wouldn't it be funny to call his friend and tell him they were coming after him! He dashed inside and dialed.

"Hey, dude, they're coming for you! Look outside. Hurry up before they attack!" Tim, a believer, was up for the challenge.

"Okay, I'll go outside and see if I can spot them."

"They're coming right at your house! It's because your house needs a paint job more than anybody's."

"Shut up." His friend tore outside with his always-ready binoculars, scanning the heavens for a view of the unearthly. He saw them.

"Man, that is so damn weird. No combustion sound."

They passed over Tim's castle and were gone.

This sighting lasted only about five minutes. Louis's growing ease with the unknown sky visitors allowed him to bring comedy into the event. What a tragedy that his government would not do the same.

Louis's best recommendation for spotting UFOs: Don't walk around kicking stones. You must look up. Watch what is going on above that you've learned to discount over the decades as unimportant. Rethink it. It's important. It's monumental. It's the new world stage.

The Plethora
Atglen, Chester County

Experience is the teacher of all things.
~Julius Caesar
Emperor of Rome,
1st century BCE

In 2005, Louis and his beautiful wife had a log house built in Atglen, Chester County. It sat on a hill in a country setting amongst the evergreens. Their two boys loved playing on the balconies under the cathedral ceilings surrounded by warm wood, and playing outside in the cool woodlands.

In 2007, Louis had a strange, if brief, encounter.

Napping in bed one afternoon, he opened his eyes to something the size of an oval dinner plate with red lights all around, flying above his bed, below the eight-foot ceiling. Just as his eyes began to focus on some of its details, it disappeared.

After that, things remained quiet for a few years. But starting in 2010, UFO activity took another upswing. It was March, and out of the northwest sky going southeast, two orbs flew over Louis's property. They had dark centers with what looked like bright white electrical flashes emanating from the center to their sphere-shaped outer shells. The shells had a slightly flattened bottom. After they zipped by, the air smelled like a welding rod. These objects visited the area a couple of times, but never loitered. They made their way across the sky without variance, and without stopping. Louis viewed these with binoculars. But never for long, since they traversed the night sky in only a couple of seconds.

The following night, he heard a horrific scream from his back deck, and witnessed a light floating around in the woods, in the area from where the scream had come. The odd thing was that there was no reason for a light to be there.

He grabbed his video camera and stalked into the woods, thinking he might catch a trespasser. He saw a bright ball of light about a hundred yards in and thought at first that maybe it was someone carrying a lantern. But why were they on his property and what would they be doing?

When he focused, the sphere looked like a star. The orb began moving slightly toward him. He dropped his camera.

Seeing something is very different than something seeing *you* and coming at you. It was time to retreat. He turned and dashed back to the house as quick as the bramble would let him. He told his wife about the wild scream, the sparkly globe, and his frayed nerves. She asked about the safety of the children—and herself and Louis. The two parents walked onto the side deck and stared into the now empty woods, bracing against the frosty March air and the chilling concept of UFOs on their property. Another paranormal night ended.

A couple of nights and a couple of beers later, Louis decided to investigate the woods where he'd seen the lights a few nights earlier. Up on his motorbike, packing a .40 caliber, he rolled into the woods about a hundred yards from the back porch, into the area he suspected had been visited. Off the bike, he revved the

engine a last time, giving potential intruders a fair warning.

Traipsing through fallen leaves, being pricked by thorny bushes, Louis started filming the area for any signs of visitation. Nearby was the tree stand his brother-in-law had built for deer hunting. It hung from branches about fifteen feet from the ground. It was a great reference point in the woods on a dark night. The camera continued to scan the leaf- and branch-covered forest floor for anything out of the norm.

That's when he saw the bones.

It was a male deer. Dead. The skeleton had been stripped of all meat. There was neither organs, nor muscle, nor brain; nothing of the insides lay anywhere. And there was no blood. The only fur was on the lower legs. The rest of the hide, in one piece, had been ripped away and piled up a few feet from the body. The tongue was still in place, something that scavengers would never overlook. There was no hair on the head. And most odd, the bones were bleached white as if they had been in the desert for decades. There was no way the bones should have been that color in so short of time in a late Pennsylvania winter.

Later, Louis brought a friend to show him the odd deer remains. No explanations were ever offered. The friend decapitated the skeleton to hang the rack in a local lodge.

Louis always carried a gun after that event and forbade his children to go near the woods at night. Still, he never felt that his family's safety was an immediate issue.

But alien instigations were not about to leave Louis in peace. Incidents continued. With company staying overnight a few months later, Louis was sleeping in the spare bedroom at the back of the house. His niece happened to be staying at his in-laws house next door, up the hill. On a Saturday evening in June, a loud whirring sound woke him around 3 a.m. It sounded electrical. He knew there was no time to get up and see it, so he decided to chalk it off as one more strange thing in his life.

Then his five-year-old son began crying in the other bedroom. His wife got up to check on his condition, calmed the boy's anxiety, and returned to her bed. Nothing unusual to report.

The next morning while Louis was pressure-washing his deck, his niece came down the road from his in-laws to visit.

"Last night," she started, "I was awakened around 3 a.m. for no reason." She looked haggard, unrested, like someone who had partied all night and couldn't find the stop button.

"Really?" Louis figured the local night spots had most of her money from the previous night. Later that day, however, it dawned on him that she must have heard the same noise that he had. Later, he explained his experience to his niece, and how his son woke up crying at the same 3 a.m. time, and how odd it all was beginning to sound.

A couple hours later he asked his son, "Remember the other night when you woke up crying? Why was that?"

His boy went eyeball to eyeball with his dad.

"Cuz of the lightning, Dad."

"Lightning. What lightning?" Louis hadn't seen any lightning. Then he remembered the bright light at cousin Charlie's. He looked hard at his son: his face, his head, his arms, his legs.

"Are you all right?" he asked his over-prodded offspring, who had backed up from the impromptu exam.

"Yes, Dad. Stop touching me."

Louis was satisfied. No sunburn at the hairline, no scoops of skin missing, no obvious implants. Dad's protective measures were still valid.

About six months later, Louis and his wife had another couple of friends staying as overnight guests. Louis slept in the back room again, dozing on his right side, facing an inside wall.

Something told him to open his eyes.

There, lying in bed next to him was the pixilating face of a humanoid being, all white, including all white eyes and a white mouth. On a more focused look, the face was not pixilating. It was formed by hundreds of bubbles. The top of the being's head was facing the bottom of the bed, so that the rest of its body extended into the wall behind the bed, and through it, and out into the night. Or so Louis assumed. There wasn't time to find out. Louis felt the terrified hairs on his head charge with electricity. He took the first action his instincts offered. He swung his left fist into the face.

It dissipated. The punch had only knocked out vacant space.

Louis sat up. His heart raced at about 169mph. Lungs pleaded for more air. Nothing like that had been so close to him since the man in black when he was seven years old. Never before had he seen such a being at close range—or any

range. And he never wanted to see it again.

From being protected by his own dad, to being a dad-protector, Louis has spent a lifetime in the shadow of the unknown. His need to be heard and his willingness to talk, paints a broad image of just one life subjected to visitations from other worlds; an impact that seems, as far as can be determined, to be a positive one.

Yet, this is not a president, king, or pharaoh. This is a regular Joe, weaving his life through the complexities of human existence. How much more weight would an alien presence have meant to a Caesar or a Salah ad-Din? What world-changing decisions might have come because of an ancient alien influence? Little by little the answers are coming.

For Louis, searching the heavens through his man-made telescope while standing on his front driveway with his sons is enough to keep him covered in stardust.

Chapter 15.
Night Terrors
Black Walnut Bottom, Lycoming County

If you're going through hell, keep going.
~Winston Churchill
British Prime Minister

Eva should have had a restful night in the family cabin, but the Universe had a more frightening plan. Huddled in Tiadaghton State Forest near Pine Creek, Lycoming County, just south of the Black Forest Trail, is the out-west-sounding recreational area of Black Walnut Bottom. The name refers to the black walnuts collected at the bottom of the tree-lined creek.

It was 1979, July, a hot, humid summer night that had the ominous feeling of getting even hotter. It had been a good day of alone time for Eva; just she and her mutt, Chauncey, enjoying the quiet of the forest and the greater quiet of less responsibility. Back home in Jersey Shore, Pennsylvania, her husband was busy with his contracting work as always. The children were at independent ages so they took care of themselves. Eva had grown weary of the routine of running

the house and was perhaps a little lonely. She just needed a breath of fresh oneness with nature to find herself again. So, spending a couple of days at the family's vacation cabin was a good idea.

Her day started with a partial hike of the forty-two mile Black Forest Trail, a return to the cabin area in the late afternoon to gather firewood, and then a shower. After dinner, despite the heat, she enjoyed the crackle of a small campfire in the fire ring near the front porch. The smoke and hot air kept the mosquitoes off balance. By nine o'clock, her body was exhausted and ready for bed. Chauncey beat her into the bedroom and settled onto his own 3' x 4' rug under the one window, which opened onto thick forest about thirty yards back from the cabin.

Eva could not sleep. The damp air pressed on her like an assailant, then oozed off her legs, arms, and neck, soaking the sheet. She felt unusually restless with every nuance in the room seeming to be a major nuisance. Even the regular sounds of camping became threats to her rest. The loud *clang* of clicking crickets, the frequent sound of airplanes traversing overhead, and the non-stop mechanical tap of the old wind-up alarm clock on the wooden night table were torturous, rather than being the usual friendly audios. Finally, she began to doze around 1 a.m.

But at three o'clock, Eva shot straight up in bed, in a daze, to the sound of a black bear roaring in her ear. As she grew to full wakefulness, she realized it wasn't a bear. It was Chauncey, frantically growling and barking, mixed with an occasional whine. The dog had its paws on the window sill that was above its sleeping rug. He peered out through the sheer curtains, his sharp vision piercing the fabric into a denser section of Tiadaghton State Forest.

Out of the bed and to the window in seconds, Eva quickly realized the source of the dog's distress. The woods outside were ablaze with an extremely intense luminescence.

"What is that?" she asked the dog, who was still yelping despite Eva's right arm around his neck. Eva ripped back the curtain for a better look. The light was about ten yards inside the woods. It seemed to be part of a machine, or device, yet the apparatus was not visible because the light was as big as a small search lamp, only ten times brighter. Despite its size and the fact that is was moving, none of the trees or bramble in the woods were disturbed by its motion. The light was moving through them, not past them. The other oddity was the entire lack of noise both from the light and the woods around it. It was as if every insect had died.

As she watched, the object moved out of the forest and entered into the clearing around her cabin. It was headed right for her!

"Oh my god," she yelled in a panic. The dog ran out of the room. Eva jumped back to her bed, knelt on the thin mattress and began to cry and pray. "Lord, let this cup pass from me!" Even kneeling, her legs quivered like a plucked guitar strings.

The light was almost at the window. As it drew closer, the bedroom log walls and everything else in the room began to turn white. Eva, too, was glowing. But there was more. She felt like she was being studied. Her entire body tingled and felt lighter. The light then moved slowly to the left away from the window. As it did the intensity dropped, shadows returned to the darkening room, and Eva sensed being released from an unseen giant hand.

The object was floating on a path around the outside of the cabin. She cautiously left the bed and baby-stepped towards the bedroom door to find out what it was doing. She clutched her night clothes in trepidation.

First the kitchen, then the living room, then the bathroom all took turns blazing in the unearthly light of the alien beam. While standing in the doorway looking into the living room, Eva again turned a ghostly white as the light's energy bleached away the stains of night. Her feet froze in place as the search lamp analyzed her existence, and then freed her as it moved around the left corner of the cabin. Eva retreated back to bed again, knelt at its center, wrapped herself in the sheet, and asked the divine for forgiveness for sins and for relief from the hellish moment she was living.

The alien light made three easy passes around the building that night for what seemed like an unending gulf of time, brightening, and then darkening the rooms, studying every molecule. Then it vanished as if it never existed.

During her vespers, Eva had been frightfully gasping for air, afraid that at any moment, something more than light would enter her cabin. But with the light gone, the crickets and katydids sounded off and the night returned to normal. Her breathing came easier.

Eva sat awake until first light, reviewing the terror of the light stalker. With facts revisited, she accepted knowing only two things. First, she knew the object was not a human-made flying device. It was not a low-flying plane or helicopter. She had lived near an airfield in Antes Fort, Pennsylvania for many years and was very familiar with the appearance of aircraft. Second, she knew she was sane.

At dawn, Eva hastily dressed and coaxed the dog out from underneath the sofa in the living room, where he had fled and stayed after the initial sighting. She then drove hell for leather back to Jersey Shore in a hysterical state. Her dog would never suffer to be put in the cabin bedroom again and would claw his way out in defiance. After that night, Chauncey always spent nights in the cabin sleeping under the sofa.

Safe at home among family, Eva related the night's events. Unfortunately, she was met with statements like "it was only a helicopter" and "you had a nightmare." But she refuted these statements with a fearsome gaze and the self-assured reasoning that she knew the difference between a helicopter and a light, and between a bad dream and the real thing.

Though no harm was done, she was glad that hell's heat was behind her.

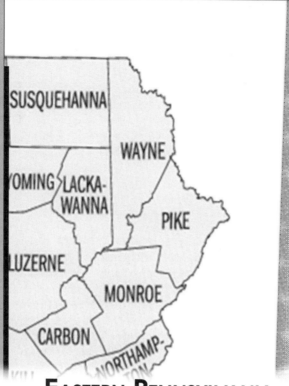

EASTERN PENNSYLVANIA

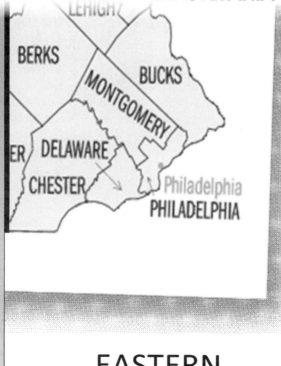

EASTERN

Chapter 16.
Alien Base Camp
French Creek State Park, Berks and Chester Counties

Gerard J. Medvec

Men occasionally stumble over the truth,
but most of them pick themselves up
and hurry off as if nothing had happened.
~Winston Churchill
British Prime Minister

So many alien devices. So many.

The Pennsylvanian woodlands are known for their intense beauty. There are still a few old-growth trees amongst the second-growth black cherry, maple, and other hardwoods in Allegheny National Forest in the northwest. I've heard strangers commenting that, dressed in its fall colors, Ridley Creek State Park in the southeast is "one of the most beautiful spots on earth."

Fall is certainly my favorite time to camp in Pennsylvania, with winter a close second. The foothills and mountains have some of the lowest elevations, for a mountain range, on earth. That is due to their being one of the oldest mountain ranges with around 480 million years of erosion. The good news is that

hiking in Pennsylvania can be a great workout without needing expensive climbing equipment. The bad news is that even when immersed in impossible yellows, reds, golds, and coppers in the canopies and ground covering of fall, occasionally there is something else.

A hiker can have tense feelings, a sense of nervousness in the deep Pennsylvania woods. Daniel Boone, born in Birdsboro, Berks County, Pennsylvania, is purported to have written about it in one of his letters. If one of America's greatest woodsmen felt uneasy in Penn's Woods, there had to be a strong reason. Whether it had to do with aliens or not, we'll never know.

French Creek State Park in Pennsylvania straddles the border between Chester and Berks

Counties. It consists of nearly 7,800 acres of continuous forest—the largest section of forest between Washington, D.C. and New York. I've hiked there hundreds of times on day trips. I've camped there on three occasions: once at a campsite and twice in one of the newer wooden cottages. These sites were in Loop C of the campground. Each trip was either in October for the forest colors, or in February or March, for the clean, cold stillness of the earth. The last trip was December 12 and 13, 2011. The exact days and years of the first two visits have been lost, but using 2004-2007 as a gage is accurate enough.

What's important is: Every time I've camped there, something unearthly happened! So, the next sentence must be: How can that be? It is impossible to bat a thousand on such coincidental, unpredictable, and outlandishly unfeasible inter- or extragalactic events! True? Untrue. Everything is possible.

When I pulled into campsite #20 in loop C, my gut twisted with the foresight that my first excursion into French Creek would be distinctive. The day was cool with expectations for a night in the high thirties. After hiking for three hours, then collecting wood for a three-hour fire, I was ready for a propane-cooked Spam dinner with black coffee. After

clean-up came the ancient rite of fire-making, as darkness fell like a stage curtain. It was a perfect toast to a day of solitude under the heavens. But camping at French Creek State Park can end up a twisted solitude.

Over the last twenty years, I've seen so much alien personal property that it has become instinct for me to search, research, and continue searching my surroundings for alien probes. In particular, I look for the circular balls of light that are the most numerous. Every electric light that dares to illuminate the human condition is under suspicion. There were several lights around, at campsites and at the restrooms that were about fifty-yards away.

Site C19 is where the one-way, graveled, loop road starts to turn left. Despite it being a weekday, there were still a dozen or so campers spread about Loop C. There was a mid-size, walk-in camper occupied by a young family on my right (facing the woods), at site C17. Across the road behind me was another family with two children on tent site C26. These were my closest neighbors.

As the fire burned in the rusty iron ring, I was getting the feeling of being watched. I sat on an upturned log facing away from the other campers, whom I was sure were busybodies, even though there was no one around. Between popping sparks and heat-waves from the logs, I scanned the woods in front of me. The campfire reflected onto moderately dense woods, with no source of light anywhere beyond the fire, irradiated the front line of trees and shrubs, but went no further. Beyond that point, the growth disappeared into a wall of blackness. This total blackout gave a feeling of being swallowed, as if only my barely-lit campsite was at the forefront of the world, and beyond laid a cavernous mouth ready to gnash me into its gut. Maybe my imagination had taken a Jeep ride into *Jurassic Park*. Maybe that type of situation in that forest was what frightened Daniel Boone. Birdsboro, where he grew up, was only two miles away, a mere one-hour stroll for ol' Daniel.

I locked down my feelings of being watched until around 8:30 p.m., when something told me to turn around. At site C26, where the family of four were camping, in front of a large tree that was behind their tent so they couldn't see it, floated an *alien globe*. It was the closest I'd ever been to one—only about forty 3yards away. However, it looked to be no more than six feet from their tent, a true concern. It resembled, well, a light, not unlike the lights near the restrooms—same color and inten-

sity, soccer ball sized. In fact, the average Mary looking at it would see nothing new. After the initial thought, she would never give it a second.

A quirk of this light was that it gave off an occasional spark. Our lights don't do that, or shouldn't. Regrets I now have about this, and all my experiences, are that I'm not a camera guy, not even a binocular guy. As a minimalist, these things I did not permit myself to own.

Damn minimalist! I was thinking. *I could really use a camera right now.*

Just then the door to the camper on site #17, to my left, opened and a mustached-man in his late thirties, in a gray sweatshirt, walked down the two trailer steps.

Thank God, I thought. A corroborator.

"Excuse me a minute," I called, never shy about being a pain in the sciatic nerve. "I'm sorry to bother you." I waved him over to me. "Do you have a minute?"

"Sure, what's up?" He seemed friendly, and started walking towards me with a no-rush-cause-I'm-out-camping jaunt.

"I want you to look at something for me," I said, pointing towards the globe. The man stopped next to me, put his hands on his hips, and looked at the alien device.

"What about it?" he asked as if we were looking at a three-year-old mule.

Wow, I thought. *Casual. He must have one of these on his mantelpiece.* "Does that light look a little strange to you?"

"No." He sounded like he thought I'd had whiskey for dinner. "There's a family on that site. They probably put it up."

"It keeps moving all the time, you see? And there's no fixture holding it up."

"It's probably on a string or something. Their kids must be moving it."

There were no people visible on that campsite.

"Do you see how it's shining all the way around, though? You can see the tree is lit behind the light. How can that be?" I was trying to press my point without being obnoxious. With each response, the man was becoming more confident that this alien property was nothing of the kind and was an increasing waste of time.

"It's just a light. Don't worry about it," he said in a pleasant, typical patronizing "guy" response meant to fix something without getting his hands dirty.

"Yeah, you're probably right," I patronized him right back without him knowing. "I'm sorry to have bothered you."

"No problem at all. You have a good night."

"Thanks, you too."

Back he went to his trailer, back to his pretty wife, cold beer, and mid-evening sitcom. By tomorrow's eggs and bacon he'd have forgotten all about the goofy guy asking him questions about the neighbor's light. Busybody. Didn't I have anything better to do? Go stoke your fire. Maybe in a couple years, when his wife kicks him out and files for divorce, or when he loses his job in a recession, the memory of that night will drift into consciousness and he'll see the globe again. The combination of clarity of hindsight and free time may point out the differences between the alien piece and the other lights that were fixed to buildings or sitting on logs. Maybe he'll think, "There *was* something different about that light."

Probably not. It might emphasize how little control he has in his life. Most guys need control. I didn't have to let years slide by; I knew what it was right then.

After the gentleman left, I walked towards the alien probe. A direct route to it was impossible, though, with too much brush between the campsites. Plus, it would also be very noisy, even dangerous. I didn't want to scare it away, as if I could intimidate geniuses from another galaxy. A couple of quick strides along the road would get me to site #26 and I'd be able to get closer, yet not too close, and watch it from the road. Four seconds later, I was at the spot directly in front of the tree where the globe was hanging out. The tree was ten to fifteen paces away at most. Unfortunately, the globe was not visible from that angle due to other trees and bushes blocking my view. I doubled back on my tracks to my original spot on the road to continue viewing the alien globe.

It was gone.

Of course it was. It/they knew we had been watching it. I also believe they knew what we were saying, thinking, and feeling. They knew if we'd been bad or good. It waited until I started moving up the road toward it to take off. As soon as I was out of sight, *zoom;* it probably went, zero to *60,000mph* in half a second. This gives the appearance of disappearance, like the Road Runner in a Warner Bros. cartoon.

But I didn't see this one leave. There was no flash of light, or roaring of super-engines. They used their modus operandi—silence. Did the globe pass through tree limbs like a ghost? Did it navigate around such irregular objects in part of a second? All unknown.

Back at my site, heat from the iron-ringed embers held my hands to quell their shaking, and rubbed my eyes to halt the questions that would keep me up all night. The embers failed.

The next day and night were earthy only. I left for home on the third morning and couldn't wait for my next camping trip to French Creek.

French Creek, first visit. Looking from site C19 towards C 26, where alien globe was seen lurking.

Fifteen Times

Gerard J. Medvec

Courage is fear holding on a minute longer.
~George S. Patton,
U.S. Army General

My second camping visit to French Creek found me a little less camping and a little more luxuriating. Autumn was present. I rented the cute, new, wooden cottage #3 for two nights. It sat with two others at the entrance to Loop C, on the left side of the road. It had double bunk beds to sleep four, a table and two chairs, electricity if needed, and a mini-front porch with a picnic table. The beauty of it was magic in your eyes.

The day was clear; the night was, too. The fire ring just off the front porch had my traditional blaze going. Right at the entrance, on the far side of the road and to my left, on site C4, was the Campground Host. They owned a large trailer with numerous exterior lights on a cord strung around the site. It looked like party time, though their site gave off only a hissy whisper of a TV playing inside. The rest of the park was quieter. There were also a couple of temporary exterior lights near the entrance to the loop to help with orientation when you first entered. It all made for a little too much light, and had the feel of a night game at a little league stadium where nobody showed up. I couldn't imagine any alien form venturing into the limelight of the forest stage. My stay this time would surely be uneventful.

Just shows how little I know about out-world civilizations.

No sooner did I get the fire going then I spied an alien globe moseying behind another trailer at site C42, to the left of the cottage about forty yards away. It was amazingly close, not five or six feet from the vehicle. Distance off the ground was about two to three feet. It was doing the traditional shimmy dance in the light coming from a window on the back of the trailer.

Was anyone inside aware of this? Should I knock on their door and tell them? How can these things move so freely amongst us and not be noticed? Three reasons work for me: camouflage, silence, and speed. Their ability to mimic our exterior lights in color and intensity gives them excellent blending capacity with their surroundings. No sound have I ever heard from any globe, no matter how close or distant I was to it. And on the times when I saw a globe and it decided to leave, it did so with better than silver bullet speed. It could vanish in the time it took two eyelids to meet and part in a fast blink.

That night's globe was as fascinating as any other, yet it was "just another alien device" that I'd seen many times. I was not bored, but I wasn't jumping out of my astronaut suit. In a moment, I wish I'd had a rocket ready to fly me to my room so I could hide under the bed.

With the area well lit, I hadn't noticed the "dead spot." This was on the right of site #1 and looked like a tunnel of shadow formed by various trees blocking out the man-made lights in just the right places. This tunnel was straight across the road from the cottage, perhaps sixty feet away. This lightless space carried back into a lightly wooded area towards Loop B.

What brought this to my attention was what I saw in the tunnel of forest shadows. It was something that rolled an icy wave up my spine and raced my heart into the Pocono 400. First, it was just a globe. It bobbed and weaved about four to five feet over the fallen leaves, higher than usual. This globe was not lit. It was a dull metallic color. From the back of the shadow tunnel, it moved towards me at a walking pace. This, too, was different, too fast. My wits went on red alert. The globe reached the near edge of the tunnel of shadow and stopped — and I froze. My heart that had been charging around my ribcage-raceway now slammed into a wall, with its survival in question.

I could now just make out what appeared to be a head. The head was to the right and slightly above the sphere. It wasn't a human head. It was featureless. In fact, it seemed more like a black energy head, rather than having skin and sinew. Even without eyes, I felt it looked at me with penetration, like a dare. The fear of that moment I had not felt for a long time. I didn't know what I should do, shouldn't do, or even what I wanted to do. My shoes seemed nailed to the wooden porch floor, and my body felt devoid of muscle. There was no running; I didn't want to. There was no shouting; not enough danger yet. There was no stone throwing; what if I'd been duped by some punk with a Halloween sense of humor.

But this wasn't funny, it wasn't a joke. It felt wildly unearthly real and too close for my sanity. If only a car or truck would drive up now and splash light on this being, as I hoped to God they would, I could see finally what the hell it was. If it was as scary as I believed it was, I could dash into the cottage, retrieve the pretend shotgun that wasn't there and I didn't own, and race back to the porch to defend my cottage to the end. (Actually, I only had my trusty six-foot, maple hiking staff for defense.)

Or the vehicle lights would show that it was just something earth-bound, tangible, easy to digest, something I didn't have to think or worry about for the rest of my life. It could be an animal carrying a basketball, or a child playing with a new, metal toy. Something I could understand.

But the head-lighted vehicle never came.

I shone my flashlight directly at it. But since most of the area was fairly well lit anyway, the weak beam washed out long before impacting the shadow. My heart was clawing at its ribbed cage, banging to get out. The "thing" and I had been searching each other for too many minutes. Action was overdue.

Since the being was not moving, I decided to make a dash for the car to get my glasses. I wanted the best view possible. I only wore my distance glasses to drive at night. But if they could help make the "thing" any clearer, I wanted them. The only issue was the car was closer to the "thing" than it was to me.

After a long breath, I shot to the car. It was parked at about a two o'clock angle from where I stood and twenty yards from the cottage. With key in hand I charged to the driver's door, unlocked it, had the glasses, and was back on the porch, proud owner of some new Olympic record. The thing hadn't budged or changed position. It just kept watching me, fraying one nerve after another. But even with glasses, nothing was clearer. It still seemed like a black, featureless head and upper body balancing this silver globe on the front of its right shoulder (not on top of the shoulder). It appeared to hold the globe, but without arms or hands. The upper body was draped in a black cloak, but it wasn't fabric. It was more like energy shaped like cloth. It didn't reach the ground, yet I couldn't see the ground where lower legs and feet would normally be. That area appeared as distortion, or empty; I wasn't sure since this "thing" was a first for me.

Once again, as a minimalist, I was camera-less. We were at stalemate. It stayed on the shadow's edge. I stayed my ground. But my usual steady continence had cracked and was disassembling like a puzzle pushed slowly over the table's edge. It was after nine o'clock. I couldn't stand on the porch all night. To stay in the cabin with the chance that "thing" could accost me as I slept made me feel desperate. My insides went into a cataclysm that flipped every organ with every other. The decision: I'm going home. It made sense. The inferior species fled in the face of the unknown. It made good sense.

My camping stuff was loaded in the minivan so fast that I can't remember doing it. My van backed up, then plowed ahead over the gravel, away from Loop C. In the rearview, the "thing" remained on guard. I hated giving up a night in nature, especially a paid one. It was precious time to me. I hoped the other campers would be safe. They always were. But alarm had sliced me open and revealed the fear in my soul to that being. Was I asking too much of myself by questioning the fear? Was it good enough that I was safe, heading home, and able to write about it years later? As the old Plymouth aimed at South Entrance Road, my stress began to drop like a hot thermometer stuck in ice. I proudly kept to the twenty-five mph limit.

But no sooner did I turn onto the road than a gleam of light hooked the corner of my left eye. I hit the brakes and looked out the driver's window.

All along South Entrance Road was either unoccupied, new-growth woods, or drop-offs. There are no hiking trails, no camping, no facilities a human could use: nothing. But I saw a soft glow not far off the road. I backed up. There, about thirty-feet off the paved road were three globes, with low-intensity, soft, blue-white lights, doing their float around routine in a small clearing.

Wow. That's six things I saw tonight, I thought. Yes, I was counting. I drove forward. Within seconds, another glow on the left. Stop again and back up. Two more globes, about the same distance into the woods, same intensity, same color. That made eight.

Oh my God, how lucky is that! I thought...or said out loud.

Forward again I went, wanting to leave danger behind, yet at this point, enamored by it. The approach to the South Entrance was downhill. About 150 yards before the entrance, there was a fifty-foot drop-off on the right. The flatland below was a private residence. I could see the back-yard. The house was lit brightly inside and out.

I slammed on my brakes. Wandering around the backyard were seven lit alien globes. Their luminosity and color matched the back light on the house. So many of them together were like watching little dancers in a pageant. Were the people in the house watching? Did they know the universe had sent its children to play in their yard? I didn't see anyone at the curtained windows. Perhaps they stood a few feet back into the room, a safer spot, enjoying the show in wonder and glee. Like most, they probably were playing on the Internet or watching TV.

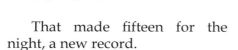

That made fifteen for the night, a new record.

Home was only a half hour to Coatesville. When I arrived, my friend, Ellen, was surprised to see me a day early. I acted out the evening events for her like a mechanical monkey whose spring was too tight. She understood. She'd seen the globes before.

Here's some insight. If on a night of no particular interest I could catch sight of fourteen globes and one "thing" in an average-sized park in one state of the United States, how many tens of thousands of these must be spread out around the sleeping side of our planet every night?

The alien presence is prolific in French Creek State Park in Pennsylvania. They seem to be permanent residents. All their base camp needs now is a tent and some Spam.

French Creek, second visit. View from site C42, about where the probe was located, looking at cottage #3.

French Creek, second visit. Author is standing on the approximate spot where the alien being stood while holding a metallic ball.

French Creek, second visit. Author on front porch of cottage #3 looking towards gate near where the alien had been standing.

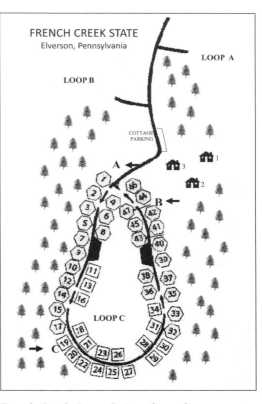

French Creek, second visit. Clearing off to the left of South Entrance Road, shortly after turning southeast off of Park Road. Several alien globes were seen here that night.

French Creek, Loop C. **A**= where alien visitor appeared (2nd visit); **B**= location of lighted probe (2nd visit); **C**= campsite C19, where Medvec had camped on 1st visit. Cottage #3 was rented on 2nd visit, cottage #2 was rented on 3rd visit by Medvec and Sarro.

French Creek, second visit. Property on the left just before exiting South Entrance. Seven bright globes hovered around the property. Artist's rendition.

An Investigator's Dilemma

Gerard J. Medvec

He that can have patience can have what he will.
~Benjamin Franklin

December 12 and 13, 2011. Notes from French Creek: 2nd day, the 13th, morning.

I'm so disappointed. No alien's stuff on night #1. In fact, the campsite, the entire Loop C, was so quiet it was weird. There were no birds, no squirrels, no chipmunks, no deer, nothing. Even the wind was absent. When standing still, there was no sound at all, except for the hardly audible white noise of distant traffic. This lasted the entire first day and night.

Mark and I had gathered plenty of wood for fire during the afternoon. Then, after dinner, we successfully lit things up. I kept looking around for alien stuff, and actually thought I saw something a couple of times. Each light that I saw that could have been alien, could just as easily have been human. Several times I followed the lights carefully for a few minutes, hoping they were not ours, but each time they proved to be either planes, the moon shining through the trees, reflections off signs, the bathroom roof, our car, or other explainable phenomena.

After a while, I grudgingly gave up mentioning lights that I saw to Mark. I'm sure he was tired of my saying, "Hey, look at that!" only to have to explain to me that we were watching the moon partially hidden behind a mist of clouds, which in turn was behind some trees, or a reflection from our parked car that was about twenty yards away.

One of the things that kept fooling me was the surprising amount of air traffic that passed overhead, and, more deceivingly, that passed by the park at a distance and altitude that kept them partially hidden behind the trees. This often made them appear like globes dancing in and out of my sightline. So, bottom line, the first night was a bust.

Today, Tuesday, started well with breakfast, a quick gathering of enough wood for a good fire, and an energetic hike on the Lenape Trail. This trail is a 5.5-mile loop that took us past Hopewell Lake, Scott Run Lake, and Hopewell Furnace. We were tired on our return, but refreshed by instant coffee and snacks. Mark carved his own hiking staff from a piece of branch we found on the trail near the beginning of our hike. My biggest concern was that since the park was empty, except for us (that's right—no other campers in the entire 7,800-acre park; the previous day's camper was gone), that the aliens would think it a waste of their time to send a probe here. I pray I'm wrong.

Expedition, December 2011

French Creek State Park, Chester and Berks Counties

Mark Sarro

An idea, to be suggestive, must come to the individual with the force of revelation.
~William James
Psychologist, philosopher

I have hunted ghosts for many years as evidenced by my list of other publications. Ghosts have been around forever. When investigating, sometimes you see them, but oftentimes nothing happens. I never dreamt you could hunt for UFOs.

And actually find them.

It was Monday, December 12, 2011, when we arrived at the park. We rented cottage #2 that sat between Loop A and Loop C of the campgrounds. Arriving about noon, we set up camp and prepared for the evening's investigation.

This was my first time camping since childhood. I was excited by the idea of being out in the woods for a possible encounter with a UFO. This was Gerry's third camping trip to French Creek. He had seen things that were wild and wonderful (as told in the prior two stories) and he wanted me to sample firsthand what this book would be about.

The afternoon passed quickly as we gathered and cut firewood and became more familiar with Loop C. It was quickly discovered that we were only one of two campers in the entire park. And we realized something else. There was no sound in the park.

It does not take a woodsman to know that every forest is alive with noise from birds, squirrels, chipmunks, the wind, etc. But French Creek was unnervingly silent. And—we did not see any of the above animals anywhere we went. Even our one fellow camper was only seen for a brief moment, and that was when he was heading out in his truck at mid-afternoon. By evening, all remained still except for the distant white noise of traffic and the occasional airplane. Nature was too quiet.

Gerry felt this might be a sign of aliens in the neighborhood. Night settled, we finished dinner and started a fire, as the partly clouded sky cleared to full star-view. I studied a sky map pro-vided by the park's office, got my bearings on the heavens, and identified Cassiopeia and Jupiter. The fire burned steadily for a few hours and we sat impatiently waiting for something to come into purview. Once the fire died down, we walked around the four loops, A-D, to see if unearthly visitors were flying around any-where. They weren't. That night ended without an episode.

The next morning found our fellow camper gone. Now we were the only campers in the park. Being the sole campers felt like a good thing. I figured that if aliens were going to make themselves known, they would probably prefer to do it without many witnesses.

We spent a good part of that day hiking the Lenape Trail, which took us, at one point, through Hopewell Furnace, a National Park adjacent to French Creek that showcases America's early iron industry. The day's activities were a workout, especially for someone who wasn't in the habit of walking over five and a half miles on a rocky trail and then sawing wood for a couple hours. Sunset brought on our routine of dinner and fire. Gerry went to gather kindling but hurried back after seeing several lights in the woods towards the back of loop C. The fire was bigger and

hotter than the previous night and someone needed to watch it.

"See if you can locate the alien globes I just saw. Stay on the road along the restrooms, and head straight back. I'll tend the fire," Gerry said as he hustled me off.

I made my way to the middle of Loop C's gravel road, standing perpendicular to the restroom's entrance area, facing the woods and waited. There were no lights. I waited for several minutes, but grew cold rather quickly as the temperature was in the low 30s that night and I was far from the fire and not prepared to be wandering off without gloves or a heavier coat. More wood was gathered on my way back to the fire.

"Did you see the lights?" Gerry asked me with a sense of eagerness and excitement.

"I did not," I stated dryly, thinking he must have mistook an airplane for aliens, again. I dumped the wood by the fire and started feeding it with the smaller pieces to get the flames burning bright.

"What do you mean? There were three of them!" Gerry took off again to look for himself. He seemed determined that we would see something that night and more specifically that I would share in the experience that he had there on previous camping trips. He went off into the night; the bouncing glow of his flashlight leading the way.

I was content to sit by the fire. I knew that if something was going to happen and that if I was meant to experience it, I would.

Gerry was back after only a nano minute. "Get your camera and binoculars and let's go! They're out there!" I hurried into the cabin and got my equipment, coat, and gloves. We zipped into loop C to the spot where he had seen the lights and ended up at campsite C32.

"Look right there! Do you see that?" Gerry exclaimed as he pointed off into the woods.

I shifted from left to right while facing the black woods that surrounded us as though we were in the belly of a great beast.

Then I saw it.

It was a spark of a light, a globe the size of a large star as viewed from earth. But this was no star. It was at eye level, out in the woods and had the color of a bronze/ orange hue. I stood there staring it down and was determined not to let it out of my sight until I was absolutely certain I could label it. The light's brightness did not waiver and it seemed stationary. I was about to dismiss it as some form of man-made light when it started to move. The brightness of the light intensified and sparks shot from it as it appeared to be panning from left to right. It was slight at first, but slowly you could see its gaze widening as it moved and turned. Suddenly, the globe turned and seemed to look right at us.

This was the brightest that I had seen it, and I could feel it was now studying us. My heart quit its usual beat and took up a faster rhythm. This was my second UFO experience. The first devices I saw in the sky over Atglen, Pennsylvania, did not hang around longer than seconds, so I assumed this one would not either. There was no time for skittishness.

I pulsed my flashlight at the globe in return communication hoping the object would come closer to investigate. Science demanded we get a better look. Nothing. The "eye" revolved away and returned to its previous business. We were being ignored.

The distance between the light and us was difficult to determine, but my best guess would be about a 100 to 150 yards. Also, we later realized it was about thirty feet up in the trees. I kept my focus on it as Gerry began scanning and searching for others. Immediately, he spotted several globes to our left with the same behaviors as the first one.

But I did not look at them. I could not take my eyes off of the first one. My mind tried to make sense of things. At first I thought of the possible illusions created by a stationary light fixed to the side of a building or pole a quarter of a mile away in dense woods. Every movement of a branch in front of this light could cause the twinkling effect and even give it a sense of movement. This was my first inclination, but I did not vocalize that, as I did not want to come across as closed-off.

My co-author had no doubts of what it was, as he had witnessed these objects many times in many locations around the country. He also knew how chameleon-like these lights and probes could be. Simply, aliens made their lights to look like ours. They wanted to blend in, go unnoticed. It would take a keen eye and patience to be able to pick them out from a sea of person-made exterior light fixtures in a city or suburban setting.

But out in the woods, they were more obvious. This, it seemed, was exactly what the globe wanted; it wanted me to think of it as nothing more than a fixed light somewhere. But as soon as it began to spin from left to right I knew that it was not attached to the outside of a restroom or a streetlight. Even with the strongest winds the light would not move that way unless it was dangling from a loose wire. And the wind was slight to nonexistent.

I tried not to blink or shift around on my feet, afraid that at any moment the vision would disappear behind an unseen limb. Maybe it would do something wondrous and I did not want to miss it. To my amazement, it began to rise up slowly into the trees as if someone ordered it skyward and it obeyed reluctantly. It rose about twenty feet and swayed left to right as it did, then it gradually made its way back down in the same fashion. The ease with which it moved showed it was independent of any tethering.

I rapidly turned the flashlight on and off again to force it to notice me. Perhaps my human behavior would annoy it and dare it to investigate. I wanted nothing more than an up-close look. Still no response.

Next, I tried to focus my camera on it and take a picture, but that was useless. There was no focal point in the darkness and the light was so tiny that the camera could not get a fix on it. When it did, the picture was a black screen. I tried with the built-in night shot, as well as with a flash, but nothing worked.

I was now frozen in place by curiosity and mesmerized by the globe's constant motion. Thirty minutes had gone by. I would have happily stood there all night to watch it. But Gerry kept reminding me to pay attention to what was going on behind us because it was not uncommon in his experience for the globes to begin to surround an observer. While nothing bad had ever come of that, there was no point taking a chance. The word "abduction" came to mind.

I turned in several directions, but did not see anything, and then quickly gazed back to the dancing light. Finally, Gerry snatched my heavy coat at the right shoulder and yanked me down the road. He wanted us to continue our search and look in other areas of the loop. He wanted me to see more. And more there was.

I did not want to go, but was in too much of an alien-revelation-fog to resist. I didn't understand why we would leave when a UFO was right before us. But Gerry insisted that there would be others. We walked to the right from site C32, continuing around the loop, making our way to the far end. I kept looking back in the direction of the original light, hoping it would be following us, but it wasn't.

Then, three more lights appeared in the woods to our left, just off site C29. Two of them moved in unison. These two were bigger, but had the same color and hue as the others. They moved up and down and side to side with no pattern or purpose. Were these two orbs hooked together?

"You see those two?" Gerry pointed to the matched set.

"They're moving as a pair," I confirmed.

"Very much like the ones I saw in Roswell, New Mexico. If they are the same, then the lights are actually windows on a small saucer."

A flying saucer? Really? The object was too far away, and the night too dark to tell if it was a ship or not. We could not walk out to the lights because the bramble was too thick. But one thing was sure: French Creek State Park was a cornucopia of alien lights. We watched them for a little while and then, reluctantly again, continued our walk. What else could be out there?

At the top of the loop near site C22, we stood in the middle of the road facing east. Above us was the constellation Orion. The sky was clearer than the previous night so the details of the stars that made up Orion were sharp and crisp. As I watched, a meteorite flashed from outside the constellation and passed directly through Orion's belt and out the other side. A day ago I would have been sure that was all it was. Now? Could it have been a UFO entering our atmosphere? I was no longer positive.

We decided to jump in the car and head to the south gate of the park to see if there were any lights visiting that neck of the woods.

Gerry had previously seen them there and was eager for a repeat performance.

There were no streetlights to guide our way. The car crawled at ten to fifteen mph towards the south gate and we maintained a watch for ominous objects that might appear in the woods on either side of us. We reached the south gate entrance emptyhanded. I U-turned and started the return trip to camp. Past the park office, past the access road to Lake Hopewell, and upwards towards Loop C we crept. About 200 yards past the access road, on a part of the street that leveled a bit, just beyond where the Lenape Trail comes out of the woods on the right, we saw another probe.

I stopped and backed up. Hard to believe there was another one floating around about one mile from the original group near Loop C. How many of these things are out here, I wondered?

This globe was the same color and size of the small globes. The glow was constant but for the occasional spark given off. The orb was at our eye level about thirty yards distant in a small clearing. It did not move with the freedom of the other lights; that is, while it shimmied back and forth, it did not leap up into the trees and fly around. It stayed two to three feet above the ground, and wavered to and fro in a non-stop motion.

I tapped the gas to lurch the car forward to see if the light would follow, but it didn't. The globe maintained its intense study of...*something*...near ground level. Since we could not distract the object from its duties, I drove hurriedly back to cottage #2. I needed a break.

Back inside our heated dwelling, we studied the park map to see what lay beyond loop C in the direction of the lights. Scott's Run Road, Scott's Run Lake, and a group camping area were southwest and west of the positions of the lights and site C32. I wanted to explore that road and area to make sure that what we saw was not being mistaken for a natural or man-made occurrence.

We drove the length of Scott's Run Road, past the lake and past the campgrounds. There were no lights to be found that could explain our sighting. We then turned right onto Fire Tower Road and made our way to Giegertown Road. On Giegertown Road, we came across houses outside the park, but none of the lights that were attached to them, or that were on the properties as lamp-posts, etc., matched the color of the UFOs. We also checked the elevation of Giegertown Road in relation to loop C. There was about a 200-foot difference (declining downward from loop C) to where these houses stood. "Our" lights were at our eye level from Loop C, putting them about thirty feet in the air. Finally, Scott's Run Road and Giegertown Road were about .5 to 1.5 miles from Loop C. It would be impossible to see any lights from the streets or houses through the thick woods at those distances.

Back at camp, we discovered on the map that a connecting trail went along the backside of Loop C. It mated the Boone and Lenape Trails with the Six Penny Trail. The Boone Trail went northwest into the Scott's Run area and the group campgrounds. I wanted to see how close the trail was and also to get a better look at the trees where my favorite UFO had been, from a perspective closer to ground-zero. This was when I saw my second meteorite. We were on the eve of the Gemini Meteor shower. Were the UFOs here to watch it, too?

Though unprepared for night hiking (we left our backpacks, provisions, and hiking staffs in the cottage), I walked onto campsite C32 and looked for an opening through the bramble that would take me down the hill and hopefully onto the trail. I pushed past sticker bushes and protruding rocks and stumbled onto the trail, literally. Gerry was fast behind me and within moments we stood side by side on the rocky trail that went to our left and right into deep darkness.

No lights, alien or human, could be seen from the trail. I made a marker so that we would know exactly where we came down the hill and onto the trail. The last thing that I wanted was to get lost at night in a 7,800-acre park. In fact, we were on the trail no more than a few minutes when we realized we shouldn't be. Being ill-prepared made it too dangerous. Up the small hill and back to the cottage we trudged.

There were five alien globes that I saw that night, plus the two meteorites. Gerry counted thirteen globes through the course of the evening, including the two that moved with "synchronicity," like windows in a possible space saucer. His thirteen encompassed my five. It was my very first experience hunting for UFOs in French Creek, and we came up with thirteen. That is an incredible number of something that many people believe do not exist. The proper questions had been asked and we tried to explore other possibilities for the cause of those lights before making the firm conclusion that they were, in fact, otherworldly. It was a massive revelation for me.

On the next expedition, I'd love to get closer.

French Creek, third visit. Entering Site C32 at night, beyond which was hovering several alien globes.

French Creek, third visit. Site C32 the next morning.

Chapter 17

The Media Disc
Media, Delaware County

Gerard J. Medvec

**The power of an air force is terrific
when there is nothing to oppose it.**
~Winston Churchill
British Prime Minister

The Air Force must have scrambled the fighters at the same time we saw the object.

The morning of December 18, 1997 in Delaware County, Pennsylvania, was cold, crisp, and clear. I left my house in Norwood to pick up my teaching-assistant coworker, Jack, at the usual 6:30 a.m. in Collingdale and then headed for another day of teenage challenges in the classrooms of Penncrest High School in Media, Pennsylvania.

Oak Avenue in Glenolden, near Mount Lebanon cemetery, part of our customary route, wasn't busier than any other workday, so I couldn't blame an inordinate amount of traffic for a metallic "reflection" in the upper left-hand corner of my windshield. It was bright, circular, and only appeared for a couple seconds. Suddenly, it elongated a tad — and was gone.

"Un-dramatic" might be the initial impression I felt. In fact, though it looked solid, I thought it must be a reflection from a vehicle behind me, since there was no oncoming traffic when the disc appeared. Of course, logic slugged me over the head with: answer — impossible. Cars behind you can't reflect in your front windshield. Still, it was a human answer that I could cling to. Yet there was no traffic when I quick-checked the rearview. The sky outside the corner of the windshield continued to fascinate me as I tilted my head at different angles like a curious dog to try to replicate the vision of what the heck I'd just seen. This was done swiftly between steering wheel jerks to keep my Plymouth minivan safely centered in the driving lane.

Then Jack, a quiet, reserved man, spoke up. "Did you see that?" he asked in an amazed fashion.

"Yeah! You saw it, too?"

"What the hell was that?" The profanity was out of character and his question had attachments of wonder, amusement, and fear.

The fact that he saw the object eliminated it from the realm of reflection since it would be impossible for a reflection to hit my eyes in the driver's seat from the upper left corner of the windshield, and hit Jack's eyes in the bucket seat three feet away, at the same angle. That would have put the object in the sky somewhere northwest of Glenolden, approximately over Media, Pennsylvania.

What we saw was quite literally "unidentifiable." It was only visible, or we only saw it, for a couple seconds. It was a circular–what? A disc? Ship? Light? Though it looked like glossy steel, we had no way of knowing anything about its composition. Plus, we could only guess at its size since we'd never seen one on the ground and there are no reference points in the sky to help us calculate.

The only certainty about this object came from an uncertain arena—feelings. It felt alien, not earthly, farther advanced. A chilling helplessness flushed my nervous system and spilled into the van between Jack and me. For a few moments, there was silence. Then we began discussing this sighting and others relating to UFOs during the rest of the ride to work. The passionate subject fueled our conversation levels skyward until it seemed the top of Everest was only a step stool away.

One thing that wasn't discussed was validation. Jack and I didn't need it. We'd seen the disc together. Neither of us need ever worry that we were mistaken, or imagining, daydreaming, or just plain screwy. We were co-witnesses forever. Whether we would be believed by future listeners of our tale, or not, their judgments would never negate our very real personal experience.

I estimated that we saw the UFO at about 6:50 a.m. By 7:10, Jack and I were escorting Special Ed students from the school bus drop-off area at the entrance to C-wing at Penncrest. Still outdoors, we walked them to the side entrance near the maintenance shop as we normally did. Along the way, we were telling the kids about our experience.

As we narrated, we pointed to the approximate area in the sky where we saw the object, which put it southwest from right overhead. There, to my surprise, were five jet fighters (two coming, I think, from the northeast—perhaps from Willow Grove AFB in Pennsylvania [no longer in operation as of 9/15/2011]; the other three coming from the southwest, maybe from Dover AFB in Delaware), all converging at the spot where Jack and I saw the UFO. There were also a couple of fighter jets following these five at a distance. The fighters were definitely flying a search pattern; that is, the two planes from the northeast flew directly at the three coming from the southwest, passing on either side of the center plane with air show accuracy. To find something in the air was their goal. They were too high and too fast to be looking for anything grounded. And if they searched, as I assumed they would, at the approximate altitude their radar gave for the disc, then I could estimate that the UFO was at around 5,000 to 6,000 feet when Jack and I saw it.

I briefly cut class and headed out the back door of C wing four more times throughout the morning to check on the search operation. The last time I looked, with our classroom teacher present, was about 10:20 a.m. They were still flying the same pattern. It had been over three hours.

Depending on your source, the American military has been either envisioned as descendants of the planet Krypton or derided as children of the damned, but one thing they are not are time wasters. The Air Force doesn't send seven jet fighters to fly over Media, Pennsylvania for several hours without a textbook reason.

Media, except for being the county seat, is a simple suburban town. The UFO they were looking for must have been solid on their radar: It was real, and it was intimidating enough to scramble some extremely expensive and decisively deadly hardware to track it down. That is reality.

Our classroom teacher, a UFO skeptic, noted at the time that the high amount of air traffic was probably due to the holiday season (despite that she could see these were military planes). She said it would be worth noting the amount of air traffic the next morning, the Friday before Christmas, to make a comparison. This we did.

The next day, Friday, December 19, 1997, the sky had only a few scattered clouds and it was easy to see if anything was flying around, especially fighter jets that exhausted white trails of smoke. There were none. In the window between 7:05 to 7:20 a.m., there were only two commercial airplanes spotted, and they were not flying in a pattern, kept quite a distance apart, and did not seem related to each other in any way, except that they were airplanes.

My conclusion: Jack and I saw something in the sky that was real but unknown, that was certainly picked up on either Pennsylvania, New Jersey, and/or Delaware Air Force radar, and that provoked an aggressive response from one or more bases in this tri-state area.

On Oak Avenue, Glenolden, Pennsylvania looking west towards Media, Pennsylvania about three blocks north of MacDade Boulevard. Mt. Jacob Cemetery is in foreground. UFO was near top of photo.

Looking NW on Oak Avenue, Glenolden, Pennsylvania, just north of MacDade Boulevard. Mt. Lebanon Cemetery is on the right. UFO was skyward on the left.

Maintenance building behind Penncrest High School, Media,
Pennsylvania. Seven jet fighters searched this confined air space
right after the sighting—for over three hours.

Chapter 18.
A Quick Study
Atglen, Chester County

I hear and I forget. I see and I remember.
~Confucius
Chinese philosopher
5th Century BCE

In September of 2011, on a cloudy gray late afternoon, Beth was chatting with a visitor in her second-floor office. It was close to quitting time and her eyes wandered more than usual towards the window, perhaps longing for the freedom of after-work hours.

One certainty was that it was not a normal sky she was watching. Something seemed different. The clouds were unlike any Beth had seen before. As her eyes drifted back and forth between interesting visitor and more interesting atmosphere, she suddenly froze in mid-sentence. From the corner of her eye Beth saw a sudden and odd light beam appear, streaming down from the heavens as if a switch had been thrown on a giant unseen spotlight. It was bright white, illuminating the small corner of an open field where several properties intersected, a few hundred yards from her building.

But despite its glow, the ground around it stayed dark. It was not a sunbeam that broke through the clouds in a last ditch effort before sunset. The sun would have been much closer to the horizon at that late hour. This beam came straight down. It was an atypical, perplexing, short-term incident that made no sense under a normal context. She tried to take a picture with her cell phone, but it did not come out clearly. After only a few seconds, it vanished as fast as it had come. Beth knew it was another alien sign.

Why was it there? How much information could it glean from a few seconds of research in the corner of a remote field? Was it looking for something? Or was it there for Beth's benefit? Could it have been a wink from the cosmos reminding her that they are always within thinking range.

Elf Magic
East Fallowfield, Chester County

A good many things go around in the dark besides Santa Claus.
~Herbert Hoover
31st President

On Christmas Eve in 1998, Beth, husband Andrew, and their son Freddie were heading to West Chester, Pennsylvania to her mom's place for a family gathering. But the journey home would make an unscheduled stop in the *Twilight Zone.*

Christmas gifts were in the back seat of the SUV, expertly wrapped with holiday papers and pretty bows and packed into plastic bags. There were enough of them to crowd right up to the three-year-old Freddie's car seat. It was a cold night with a low cloud cover. The time was a little after five o'clock.

The family was driving east on Strasburg Road by the Brandywine Middle School. As they cruised to the stop sign at Route 82, the car crested a small knoll, giving them an unparalleled view of quiet, semi-rural East Fallowfied, Pennsylvania. As the town name implies, the entire area is, or was, farmland — very few trees anywhere, leaving wide-open vistas of soft rolling hills and massive sky.

Normally, Andrew would have coasted through that stop sign on a Christmas Eve with zero traffic anywhere. But that night, he stomped on the brake and white knuckled the steering wheel. He and Beth gaped at the clouds ahead. There, a star-white ball of light streamed across the sky. It streaked silently over Strasburg Road, no more than 200 feet up. Unlike a meteor, it did not angle down towards earth, but kept a parallel trajectory during its brief shot through the atmosphere.

"Whoa, what the heck was that?" Beth exclaimed.

An excited adult male voice answered from the back seat.

"Look, there's an alien!"

But there was no adult male in the back seat, just a three year old and a pile of gifts. Heads swiveled, eyes made contact. Beth and Andrew sucked in their breath as they realized that they recognized the voice. It's Woody!

Among the Christmas presents were two toys for their son, tightly wrapped and bowed, in a bag. They were the sixteen-inch talking dolls Sheriff Woody and Buzz Lightyear from the *Toy Story* movie. The Buzz Lightyear toy was battery-operated. But the Woody toy was not battery operated. There was an old-school pullstring on Woody's back. The string had to be pulled out six or seven inches to get the toy to talk. The toy boxes had never been opened. They were wrapped solid.

"What the...?" said Beth and Andrew in unison.

Their three year old had not impishly broken into the wrappings, opened the Woody box, and pulled the string at just the right moment, to have Woody say by the wildest coincidence the only reference to "aliens" in his mechanical repertoire of over fifty phrases. No, that's not what happened. There was no disturbance in the back of the car. Freddie was strapped securely in his seat, gazing back in wonder at the astonished faces on mommy and daddy. The presents were untouched.

"Oh my god. What the heck just happened here?" Beth asked as if Santa had just passed them at 200mph in a '68 Plymouth Barracuda.

"We saw something in the sky," said Andrew slowly, grasping for handles.

"Then Woody talked to us, and said it was an "alien," Beth added with equal timbre, trying to rationalize.

"Let's get out of here before the ghost of Christmas past jumps on the hood," Andrew concluded, swiftly slamming the gear shifter into drive and punching the pedal.

They sped down Strasburg Road at a higher than legal pace, eager for the lights of West Chester and some of her mom's figgy pudding. Since that night Beth and Andrew have seen other UFOs. It has changed the way they walk and drive. They constantly watch the skies now, enduring only the occasional stumble or swerve. They know there is more in the dark than meteors and sleighs, and while they are never afraid, they are hoping the magic is kept to a minimum.

Chapter 19.
A Few Very Short Stories

A collection of short descriptions of sightings—courtesy of International UFO Museum and Research Center, Roswell, New Mexico; The National UFO Reporting Center (www.ufocenter.com); and Filer's Files.com.

Allentown, Lehigh County
August 24, 2010; approximately 10:25 p.m.

It was reported that a large, silver triangle, about sixty-five feet across, flew at about 100 feet above the ground, over the area. It had bright, round lights at each tip.

Bloomsburg, Columbia County
January 26, 2006; approximately 11 p.m.

Four witnesses studying the Orion Constellation noticed that one bright, star-like object was moving towards them. Observing through binoculars, one witness described the object, which was now directly over their house, as diamond shape with a bright light in each corner.

They watched the object for about ten minutes.

Elizabethtown, Lancaster County
August 12, 2011; approximately 9 p.m.

A woman saw a UFO flying towards her from the west. She was on her back porch. The object turned north about 200 yards from the house. She described the UFO as a disk with a dome. At the bottom of the dome there were windows with white lights. The lower half of the disk was spinning slowly and had large bright blue, red, and white lights. It traveled in silence. The lights reflected off the tops of the trees which were ninety feet off the ground.

The sun was setting, the moon was up and almost full, the skies were clear.

Doylestown, Bucks County
January 1, 2011; approximately 10:25 p.m.

The witness was on South Clinton Street when he noticed numerous bright objects in the eastern sky. There were about twenty objects moving from south to north. They were on a semi-circular trajectory. They gained altitude as they moved further away and disappeared after about ten minutes.

Scranton, Lackawanna County
June 1, 2008; approximately 4:20 p.m.

A dark object was seen flying from north to south near the local airport. The witness lived near the airport and was used to seeing planes overhead on a daily basis. The dark object moved slower than the planes that were flying nearby at that moment. The object had no wings. Its shiny metallic surface reflected the sun. No sound came from it. The object was flying lower than the planes. It was smaller than them, but bigger than a car.

Quakertown, Bucks County
June 25, 2010; approximately 6 p.m.

An object shaped like a flying, white cigarette flew over a witness's yard, northbound. The item was about the size of a large shopping center and appeared to fade away at the edges. This is a congested area, not far from the former Willow Grove Naval Air Station. The object moved left and right smoothly, and was observed for about sixty seconds. Binoculars were used. About ninety minutes later, a neighbor verified that he too saw the flying cigarette traveling westbound.

Philadelphia, Philadelphia County
May 10, 2008; approximately 6 p.m.

From a top-floor apartment window, facing east, near the Delaware River, halfway between the Betsy Ross and Tacony-Palmyra Bridges, a witness saw a giant boomerang flying about 200 yards away. It had three amber headlights and six bright white lights under each wing.

Northeast Philadelphia Airport, Philadelphia County
June 17, 2011; approximately 10 p.m.

Two witnesses walking near the airport, watched for twenty seconds as an orange-red object hovered over the area, then sped away at high speed.

Lackawanna County
July 4, 2008; approximately 11 p.m.

From their patio, two witnesses saw an orange light hovering in the sky. It was not an airplane since they don't hover. Nor was it a helicopter. Suddenly, it shot upward and disappeared into space. Five minutes later, it was back. It was triangular with one orange light in the front. After only seconds, it disappeared again upward. A few minutes later, three appeared, each in a different part of the valley where the witnesses lived, but observable from the patio. Seconds later, all three vanished.

Kutztown, Berks County
November 23, 2009; approximately 11 a.m.

Three witnesses were flying paper airplanes near a pasture when they saw a fireball coming through the clouds at rocket speed. At first, they thought it was a burning aircraft or a meteor. But the object began to slow down, yet maintain its spherical shape, and straight trajectory. The fire went out and the object was gone.

Easton, Northampton, County
August 22, 1966; approximately 10:15 p.m.

A woman was driving her daughter, her daughter's friend, and her son home. They were heading west and came to a stop sign. Looking up, she saw a huge orange-red light. It was hovering. Then the object completely changed color and shape. Now it was disk-shaped and, in the center of the disk, it looked like someone had put a grapefruit half there. The object then turned back to orange-red and descended in their direction. It moved with a fluttering motion like a leaf falling from a tree. The woman became frightened. She quickly drove the last block to her house. The four witnesses got out of the car and began making a racket to attract neighbors and family members to the odd sight. Her husband came out the side door to join them. The object changed shape and color again. Now it was shaped like a cone or fan. Then suddenly it closed in on itself (like a fan) to a thin streak of light and disappeared southwest in seconds.

West Chester, Chester County June 10, 2007; approximately 9:30 p.m.

While sitting on her back deck, a woman and her boyfriend watched thousands of sparkling, white lights floating near a cluster of trees near a small waterway. Originally thought to be lightning bugs, the lights did not blink like the bugs. The lights maintained a planned geometric pattern, unlike nature. This was also not an aircraft.

Chapter 20

UFO University
Rosemont, Delaware County

**True, a little learning is a dangerous thing,
but it still beats total ignorance.**
~Abigail Van Buren,
a.k.a. Pauline Phillips
Founder of advice column "Dear Abby"

That spring night, Mary Louise Franklin saw the unforgettable.

"I wish I'd never seen it," she said, half to herself, as if wishing the memory away.

The year was 1963. The Beatles had just recorded *Please, Please Me,* their first album for Parlaphone Records. Later that summer, the bikini would make its American debut, and by the end of November, President Kennedy would be dead. Gas was $.39 a gallon, a loaf of bread was $.22, and a new Buick ran about $2,000. It had been two years since Betty and Barney Hill of New Hampshire reported being abducted by aliens.

"I was a senior at Roselyn University, a private, all-girls school in Rosemont, Pennsylvania," Mary explained. "The campus was luxurious, having been a former estate. The main build-ing was all stone with imposing, round towers on every corner. I lived in a first-floor room in Mally Hall, one of the newer dorms."

Mary had been studying for hours for the next day's exam. By 8 p.m., she was book-weary, brain-fatigued, and in need of clean air. A stroll in the fresh spring night would be nice. So out the front door she went.

Located before the dorm was a large open space with a flagpole.

I saw a bright light and looked up. There, hovering fifty to seventy feet above the flagpole was an oval-shaped machine. Roughly the size of one and a half Buicks, it had brilliant white lights spaced a couple feet apart all the way around the sides of the oval. A barely audible hum permeated the air. One could sense that there was intelligence manning the craft, and you felt that you were being observed.

Initially dazzled by this motionless miracle, Mary quickly recovered and sprang into action.

There was always a nun on duty in each dorm, so I ran back in to get her. I told her to hurry outside. Being young and less cautious, I was screaming like I'd just seen Elvis Presley, "Come on, come and see this ship! You're not going to believe it!" It was more exciting than scary. I ran through the halls shouting for everyone to come outside and see this "thing." I don't know how many of the other girls I also pulled out, but it had to be about forty or fifty.

We stood in a crescent formation in front of the dorm and just gaped at the machine. I knew that we all had the same feeling of someone inside this vessel watching us. I couldn't tell for sure how high it was in the air, but I was seriously waiting for a ladder to come down.

The vision overhead was so compelling that all I did was stare. For a full twenty minutes, I looked the machine over, again and again. It was fascinating. It was as if nothing else existed, nothing else was important at that moment. I can't say what the other girls were doing. Even my friend, Janet, who was next to me, was quiet and, I assume, doing nothing but watching the saucer. We were mesmerized, almost hypnotized! After twenty minutes, the flying machine took off at amazing speed! In two seconds, it was gone over the hillside.

Everyone ran inside and someone, probably the nun, called the Civil Air Patrol. There had been many sightings in those years, especially in the Midwest. I followed up with the sister about the Civil Air Patrol phone call and heard that they had said, "Thank you. But we haven't seen anything." The saucer was so low that I'm sure it was under the Air Force and commercial radars. That was the end of the Civil Air Patrol's involvement.

When we were back in our room, all the feelings that had backed up behind the original excitement oozed out of us like the *Blob*. We talked about how frightened we were and how spooky the ordeal felt. My roommate and I were afraid that night. Our room was on the first floor. Since I

was the one who spotted it, we were afraid they might come in the building and "get us" in our room. We thought they might come in through the glass, or something.

That spring night "higher education" took on greater meaning, greater than books can reveal, greater than universities can offer. The UFO was its own profound, silent lecture; the lesson—far, far reaching.

Chapter 21.
Fate Steps In
Atglen, Chester County

Mark Sarro

**Although our intellect always longs for clarity
and certainty, our nature often finds uncertainty fascinating.**
~Karl Von Clausewitz
Prussian soldier and
German military theorist 19th Century

I had never seen a UFO before, not until the wee hours of November 6, 2011. I was driving home from the Lancaster, Pennsylvania area after playing a show with my band MK Omega at the Laserdome (a laser-tag arena and rock music venue). It was a little after 2 a.m. when I had turned south onto Route 41 from Route 30.

This event happened in the midst of a very busy time for my co-author and I. We were wrapping up the stories and manuscript for our book, *Ghosts of Delaware*. Less than a week before, on Halloween night, Gerry had witnessed an amazing UFO incident along Route 1, near Odessa, Delaware, on our way home from that evening's ghost investigation on Cape Henlopen. (You can read about that adventure in *Ghosts of Delaware*.)

Thoughts of UFOs were beginning to float in my head now that the ghost book was done. I was opening up to the possibility of odd things happening in the night skies above me. Gerry influenced that process, as he brought me to a state of awareness with numerous stories of his firsthand UFO experiences around the country. The recurring theme was "keep looking up," and so this became my mantra as I drove home on these late evenings from our band performances and other events.

This was the case on that November evening when I looked into the night sky beyond my dashboard. Gerry also talked about how intelligent these beings were and the capabilities of their technology. One of his theories is that they can monitor and perhaps hear us from great distances. This idea seemed a bit out there, but as

I would soon realize, it was not such a wild and out there way of thinking!

November 6th was a clear night; the stars were bright, filling the skies end to end. Route 41 was absent of traffic, dark and lined with trees at different spots on either side. I began a mantra: "I wanna see a UFO. I wanna see a UFO," and repeated it over and over again as I drove slowly onward. My marrow was on edge. Something was about to happen.

I hunched forward, both hands strangling the steering wheel, and becoming more wide-eyed as I peered through the windshield wishing for a miracle. I kept one eye on the road and one eye in the sky, slowly scanning from left to right as the tree lines opened up to reveal rolling hills and fields to my left. I looked at the clock. It was 2:05 a.m.

Then it happened.

Out the windshield in the eleven o'clock position was a burst of light that was bigger than a full moon. Then five other lights broke off from it in the center and at the same time all lights went dim.

Blink, blink my eyes went as I stopped mid-mantra. "I wanna see a...what was that?" I asked myself aloud in the car. My mind immediately raced towards a rational explanation.

"Fireworks? A meteorite? What?" I asked myself over and over again. I began going through all the possible scenarios in my mind.

"Ok, fireworks. Hmm, well. It's after 2 a.m. on Sunday morning, in the middle of a sky, where at landscape level there are fields and very few houses... Fireworks, really? I don't think so. There was no smoke, no sound and at 2 a.m.? I think I am the only person awake in this entire area," I mused.

"A meteorite. I have seen plenty of meteorites in my lifetime, both on video and in person and I know that with the brightness and intensity with which this just flashed that there needed to be a trail of smoke, but there was none."

The color of the light was a hot white that would be typical for a meteorite entering and burning in our atmosphere. The size of the initial flash before it broke off into five directions was one that I believe for a meteorite. But it would have left a trail of smoke or something of that nature. Also, when it broke off into five smaller lights, they all went into different directions. With the forward momentum of the object and gravity, I believe that if it were a meteorite, the five smaller objects would have continued in the same direction and not veered off into different opposing directions like it did. The behavior of these smaller lights is what initially led me to rationalize that it was possibly fireworks.

Can I say with absolute certainty that it was a UFO? Yes, because it was truly an Unidentified Flying Object. I don't know for certain if it was some type of alien craft or ship, but I can't help but wander down that path after observing how the smaller lights took off in different directions, as if propelled, and then simultaneously extinguished.

It was shortly after this event that I began researching more into the different types of UFO phenomena and sightings that have been reported all over the world. I needed to understand better what I had seen as well as get a handle on what was seen by so many others. The one thing I learned was that there had been numerous sightings in the skies around Atglen, Pennsylvania.

A few weeks later, on the last day of November, Gerry and I drove up to Atglen to trace my steps back from Route 41 to the area where I had the experience. We drove along and came slowly to the same open space in the road where I had seen the objects, and much to my amazement and shock, it was in the exact same location as the sightings reported by the owner of the property in that area. It appeared that my sighting was one of many in that general location. At that moment, Gerry and I decided that we would pursue the neighboring property owner in hopes of getting his story and to be able to "camp out" on his property for some sky watching of our own.

I know what I saw and I know now in my mind what I think it was. I have replayed these events over and over again and have discussed them in great detail with Gerry as to what exactly it was that I saw. Coupled with the research and other eyewitness reports, it has become abundantly clear to me that what I saw was not in fact fireworks or a meteorite, but something else altogether.

Chapter 22.
The Light Beings of Lady She
Sadsburyville, Chester County

When one has the feeling of dislike for evil, when one feels tranquil, one finds pleasure in listening to good teachings; when one has these feelings and appreciates them, one is free of fear.
~Siddhartha Guatama
The Buddha

Thought at one time to be strictly an angelic group, upon research, Lady She discovered that the "Light Beings" were thought by many to be a star-dwelling species. The Light Beings considered themselves part of the UFO community—and not the only group with whom she would be in touch.

One might think that ETs would be sending messages to presidents and prime ministers, or trying to influence priests, ministers, or rinpoches. It turns out that the person who is most properly in tune with the Universe is their usual choice, be they from Philadelphia, Pittsburgh, or Sadsburyville, a quiet hamlet on Route 30 just west of Coatesville in Chester County, Pennsylvania.

The Light Beings had first contacted Lady She through her dreams. They requested her to become more involved with the world of the paranormal and the greater Universe. This group of aliens (which she saw in her mind's eye as tubes of light) then began channeling information through her. Channeling is the practice of serving as a medium through which a spirit, or alien guide, purportedly communicates with other people or groups of people.

It was the specific nature of this group of Light Beings to assist in raising vibrations in individuals and for the masses on earth in order to get them ready for times coming. Raising vibrations is supposed to elevate a person's levels of consciousness, and could be done, She was told, in many ways for a varied population.

The Light Beings went about describing and putting those ways to use through Lady She. She has worked with "them" to help people with increasing their personal vibrations since 2008. It was not easy work because the Light Beings did not wish to talk about anything but vibrations, and unlike other channels, they do not provide attunement (the awareness of self-empowerment), information for, or about, the future, or specific advice on daily living (no lottery numbers!). They only discussed vibration.

The Beings sent Lady She messages sometimes that seemed important to her. However, they often kept that information cryptic because it was not the right time (from 2008 until 2012 and beyond) to release any kind of discussion about what was coming to the general public.

So why did they send the information in the first place? There was no answer for that. They were there for her in times of stress and woe as a comfort, but not as healers or as givers of answers. And as much as she did request specific answers for particular problems, it was always in vain. This was the life of Lady She.

Someone claiming that aliens communicate with them through their dreams may seem too far from home plate for most people. But this claim is nothing new.

Many a person filmed in interviews since the 1950s and '60s claimed that they were in contact with aliens either by telepathy or by physical means. Validating such claims is nearly impossible. One's best, perhaps only, bet for accepting someone's claim about alien communications may be verifying the credibility of the claimant. In the case of Lady She, credibility is high.

May 26, 2010; approximately 7:22 a.m. Parkesburg, Chester County

Lady She was on her way to work, turning left off Route 30 onto Route 10 towards Route 372 in Parkesburg, Pennsylvania. She looked out her driver's side window and saw a metallic, white, triangular-shaped object turned sideways. Its top point reflected light from the morning sun. It appeared to be a thin triangle, but while triangles had sharp geometric lines, the lines of this craft were rounded, almost bulging at the sides and front. It did not resemble the triangular planes identified as Air Force craft or even other UFOs. And the white was so brilliant that it nearly glittered. The sun was positioned at about 10 on a clock face and the ship was southwest at about 4. Immediately, as she looked at it, it winked out of sight.

Right away, her mind told her that she did not see the object, but she quickly pushed that thought away, knowing how the brain interferes by immediately denying something that was real because it is too far outside the brain's realm of normality. She knew what she saw.

Arriving at her work, another worker came to her office to say that she, too, had seen something strange that sounded like the same object. Corroboration between witnesses felt good.

The best part of this sighting for Lady She was that the night before, She had talked with the Light Beings and had asked for a sighting. Due to her getting so much information from them, she felt she needed a dose of physical evidence to once again confirm that it was the Light Beings she was hearing. She was comfortable going on faith with the Beings up to a point, but still needed a morsel of the 3-D from time to time. She had asked to see a UFO or an alien, or something tangible. The triangle was bigger than a morsel. It was a real spaceship.

While at work, thinking about the sighting, she wished that she could have seen it for a longer time, maybe see the lights on it, or view it more closely. A voice from the Light Beings in her head laughed out loud and told her that she was never satisfied.

They were right.

November 9, 2010, approx. 4:58; p.m. Atglen, Chester County

Robert had called three times before Lady She was able to call him back. While employment tasks at the office were keeping her head spinning, with each voice mail, Robert's voice grew more anxious. He said he had fallen asleep at his computer and had a "Mantis" dream that included Lady She. And it scared him. Scared him enough that he needed to tell her about it *right now*.

The Mantises are a reputed alien civilization who, in appearance, resembles the earth insect, the preying mantis.

Finally, she found a quiet moment to return his call. Robert's dream with Lady She in it was as bizarre as the creatures it was about:

> There was a flat orange plateau. A group of hooded, dark-robed Mantis individuals were there facing Lady She and two other Mantises on either side of her. The three of them were wearing hooded, white robes. It was a face-off. The two Beings with She nodded to the leader on the other side, acknowledging him as an observer. The Mantis on She's right then handed her a plastic-look-

ing rod of about one foot in length. The Mantis on her left moved a tentacle-arm towards the clear blue sky and a screen appeared in that sky before them. The screen showed three triangles followed by a dash and two purple-filled circles. They asked She to choose the correct shape. Her dream image chose the center triangle. Everything else on the screen dissolved. The middle triangle opened, showing an alien language and then a translation device from somewhere began to translate that language into English. She could hear: "All this you see will be different and will change, and will not be the same world, and this will come soon." Then the dream faded away. While still asleep, Robert asked what was meant by "soon?" Urgency began to fill his senses and the words "very soon" ballooned his essence to a near explosive discomfort.

He awoke and called She instantly. The two friends discussed all that this could mean at great length, but could, of course, come to little understanding of it.

On her way home that day, She traveled north on Route 10. As she reached the Wal-Mart around 4:58 p.m., she noted out her front driver's window in the air at 12 high, a silver metallic, vertical, rectangular shape. She started talking out loud to herself, "What is that? It's not a plane, no lights flashing. And it's not moving at all!" As she moved towards the traffic light crossing Route 10 at Route 30, she watched the shape for about ten seconds, hovering. Then she tore her attention back to the road for just a second and then back to the air. The craft was gone.

The good news—She had seen another UFO. Other good news— she had a Mantis inspired dream to ponder.

November 11, 2010; approximately 3:30 a.m. Sadsburyville, Chester County

Upon going to bed, Lady She made a mental note to her Light Beings that she would like, if possible, to stay a bit more connected to the Mantis folk in her dreams, and she would work hard on remembering the dreams they sent. She fell off to sleep.

At about 3:30 a.m., she awoke to a soft tapping on the wall next to her bed. The tapping was nothing new; it was a signal for her from the Light Beings, but it still tended to catch her off guard and always kept her wondering.

She laid still and acknowledged that she was hearing the taps and asked what the message was. But no answer came to her mind or heart.

Then the smoke alarm started with its "one beep every fifteen seconds show." This had not been the first smoke alarm "message" she'd gotten over the years. In fact, over the prior two weeks, off and on, she and her husband had been awakened at 3:30 a.m. by a different smoke alarm every time. All the batteries had been checked since her husband had a gadget to do that, and were in tip-top condition. There were no mechanical problems and no reason for them to start and stop so suddenly. She got up and went out to stand in front of the alarm. She was so tired; she just reached up and yanked the alarm off the wall (after making sure the house wasn't on fire!). The battery was removed, and She walked back to her room, muttering, "Tell me in a dream; I don't get the alarm message." If later a message had come, she could not remember.

December, a Weekday, 2010; approximately 4:15 p.m. Atglen, Chester County

The first UFO sighting at the workplace for Lady She was at dusk with the sky emanating a combination of pinks and purples. There was also one large cloud outside her second-story office window that did not seem to belong in the sky. It resembled the odd formations that she had seen on the Internet that claimed to mask UFOs.

At 4:15 p.m., she was again on the phone talking about UFOs, when out of the strange cloud popped a single light. She turned away from the window, not wanting to think that while she was talking with someone about UFOs, a UFO was coming into view. But curiosity was too strong. She turned back to the glass. The cloud and the round, bright light were still there— stationary in their original spots. Then the light vanished and the cloud disappeared.

A slight scream started from Lady She, but she swallowed it. Her phone partner was filled in about the miracle of the previous moments. She had talked about them, and they had come.

August 11, 2011; approximately 10:40 a.m. Atglen, Chester County

A strange, stationary cloud began to form outside Lady She's office window. This was the second time in nine months. It was strange enough that she stopped her work to think about it being strange. Elongated with jagged edges, it did not move or "act" like any cloud was supposed to act. Immediately, She felt a compulsion to go down to the warehouse to tell her co-worker/shipper and UFO believer, Cynthia, to "watch that cloud." This was highly unlikely behavior for Lady She, who kept to her office duties and did not usually share paranormal tales with fellow employees. Finally, she dismissed the feeling to talk to Cynthia, stayed at her desk, and got back to work. But about five minutes later, She got a call from her friend Paco who was also an alien sympathizer. This friend started chattering about a UFO story he had recently been told. She would interject with pieces of information about her strange cloud that was still outside the window.

At 10:49, She cut her friend off and told him to hold on for a new development. The cloud suddenly severed in half and a small sliver of a moving craft, silver and shiny

in color, could be seen traveling west. She squinted trying for a closer look because it was not an airplane. Then, *poof,* it winked out of existence. The cloud also dissipated in seconds, leaving only blue sky.

This was the second UFO incident to occur outside that work window, giving She the feeling of working in front of a portal.

Peculiar Side Bars

Lady She relayed her stories for this book both with a face-to-face interview and with written notes typed into her computer in 2012 in preparation for the interview. As she typed the "December, a weekday, 2010" incident relayed in the prior story and tried to save it, she noticed that she had written another experience labeled November 10, 2010. She opened that file to see if she had already written the story and had forgotten about it. That file was on a different mind/body/spirit topic (vibrations), but—at the end on the document in the middle of the page, with no text near it above or below, was a large smiley face icon. She didn't know how to make a smiley face in Microsoft Word, and had no reason to put one there. How did it get there? Was it, as she felt, an amusing response from an intelligent out-worlder to her working passionately on her UFO stories?

Another odd side bar: As She was typing the above sidebar, the UFO person who had called her during the "December, a weekday, 2010" story called again.

How tight is the connection between like-minds? Never let anyone tell you coincidence is real. It was *not* a coincidence.

October 2011 Sadsburyville, Chester County

Lady She was researching UFOs at home late one night on the net, and was listening to various *blogtalkradio* interviews about the subject. (www.blogtalkradio. com.) One particular radio program had a different approach to the phenomenon and was accusing aliens/star beings of being negative entities. This person talked a good show and She found herself wondering if she was backing the "wrong side," believing that aliens were mostly good guys. This related specifically to the Zeta beings who many believe have a desire to control us.

As she pointed and clicked around the screen she suddenly got a push from inside her soul to channel messages from the Light Beings. This would often happen when the Light Beings were "listening in" and had something to tell her. Similar to an act of meditation She relaxed her body and the Light Beings asked her if she would allow a Zeta to come to her in her dreams that night to discuss the program she was listening to. The Zeta, apparently, wanted to discuss these new defaming allegations that she had been considering.

"Wow. How cool is that?" She thought as a wave of adventure washed over her. After finding out that she would be safe in doing so, She agreed to allow the Zeta into a dream.

So finally, the computer was shut down and She began her bedtime ritual. The room was dark, her husband was already sleeping, and she was moving about with a small flashlight. She got into bed, flicked off the flashlight, and laid her head on the pillow.

Still awake, she heard three loud knocks on the wall by her head. She freaked, knowing somehow that a Zeta was coming to call. Inside her head, she screamed. "Noooooooo! You said in a dream! I don't want to actually *see* you!"

That was the last thing she remembered. She woke the next morning to a feeling of euphoria and had no negative concerns at all about the Zetas that she'd had the prior night. It was so strange, but she knew that she'd had an experience—but Lady She couldn't remember what it was; nothing beyond aliens knocking on the walls.

Did the Zetas reassure her in a dream that their intentions toward earth were friendly? Or did they brainwash She into believing, so that she would be left her to pass disarming information on to the rest of us?

It would not make sense for aliens to beat around the bush about "taking over" our simple planet. Anyone advanced enough to communicate vast distances by entering into people's dreams, or even showing up in person, could easily conquer our world with minimal effort. On top of that, there is a rule on earth that, while it is unknown if the rule applies to other worlds, says: "What goes around comes around, three times over." Most people have heard of this ancient rule. Most people never adhere to it. This rule never varies, never lets up for anyone. Once you see this rule in action in your life, the human experience changes forever.

If this rule exists in other places, then the aliens would be wise enough to know it and stick to it. Why denigrate helpless humans just to have something three times as awful smack your gray, or Zeta face? Lady She believes now that those Zetas here in this time frame of 2010 and beyond have good intentions— at least those knocking on *her* walls!

Chapter 23.
Invasion
Coatesville, Chester County

Gerard J. Medvec

There is nothing that man fears more than the touch of the unknown. He wants to see what is reaching towards him, and to be able to recognize or at least classify it. Man always tends to avoid physical contact with anything strange.
~Elias Canetti
Nobel Prize in Literature 1981

The event that started on January 3, 2007 took UFOs to a new level in my life and maybe in the lives of all earthlings. Somebody once told me to keep a journal of all the remarkable paranormal things that happened to me in my otherwise typical lower middle-class life, so I did. Like most journalists, faithfulness to my little green book was total in the beginning. But after a couple years, the romance waned. I even cheated on my green friend with movie theaters, weekend dances, and plenty of restaurant dinners. Finally, I quit. For seven years I didn't use enough ink to fill a dash. That didn't mean there was nothing to write about. Au contraire. The paranormal was poppin'. I just wasn't pressed to pen it.

Then the invasion came. And I wrote like a crazed monk in a haunted abbey.

Alien invasion. Those words, stuffed into common usage back in the 1950s, meant terror to believers and absurdity to the rest of post-World War II humanity. Thanks to copious sci-fi "B" movies, countless "space man" magazines, and closed-minded cold war attitudes, most of the aliens out there were war mongers that would devastate our planet, and/or deceiving infiltrators that adopted our looks, walked among us, and enslaved us one by one.

Alien invasion. Little did I know how it really worked. After January 3, traditional beliefs were a joke. It happened on Eleventh Avenue in Coatesville, Pennsylvania. The street climbs a steep hill south of Route 30. A nice little red brick twin house was my home. The house enjoyed a tranquil neighborhood with its sibling on the right usually absent of renters, and the alleyway on its left seldom traversed by traffic. There was a magnolia tree in the front left corner of the side yard and a mature Japanese maple further back, partly shielding the side of the house.

My friend Ellen rented me the middle bedroom on the second floor. Its perky yellow walls with white ceiling and trim, dark walnut-stained entrance and closet doors, with a medium gray rug, supported a cheerful atmosphere. The three large one-over-one windows, each separated by thick white trim about a foot wide, had no window treatments. Day and moon lights had easy entry. The plaid sofa, where I slept, was against the left wall as you walked into the room. Being on a hill, the view out the windows was unobstructed sky, but for the upper bare branches of the Japanese maple, about ten feet from the glass.

January 3rd was a night of few clouds, and the street lamp near the front left corner of the property gave off a smooth, low glow that spilled easily into the big windows. Although the upper corners of the room were as murky as lampblack, there was no need for a night light.

I sleep better than dead men, but around 2:25 a.m., my eyes suddenly shot open. I was completely alert, on guard—and watching a weird phenomenon.

Right outside the center window floated a spinning alien device. It was dark, metallic gray, no bigger than a two-gallon bucket, and was either spinning very fast, or out of focus in our environment, or something else. Silently, it hovered outside the lower pane of the middle of the three windows, close to the glass so it was easy for me to see. The street lamp was doing a great job illuminating this "thing" and the leafless Japanese maple branches behind it.

I'd seen this probe before. It had been caught on video by a number of different people and shown on TV at various times. Firsthand for me was better. A sure sign of its intelligence was that when I woke up, the probe knew it. It backed up a few inches, as if my eyes opening startled it. Then it moved slowly to my right and hid behind the one-foot wide mullion.

I got out of bed and went to the far-right window. It only took seconds for me to trek the twelve-foot wide room, but the probe had already used the cover of the mullion to back away from the house, hoping I wouldn't see it. It was now close to the maple tree's upper branches, about ten feet away.

"Ellen! Ellen, wake up! Ellen, hurry, come in here," I yelled in a voice strained from excitement, fear, and yearning, with a touch of courtesy.

While I watched, the object moved slowly from the tree back towards the house, but at a sharp angle upwards to the right. In a few seconds it disappeared over the roofline, out of sight.

"What's wrong?" Ellen asked as she entered my room, four steps too late.

"A UFO was here, floating outside the window!"

"Oh my god! What did it look like?" Ellen's instant acceptance was not naiveté, but based on her own experiences with alien sightings. We talked passionately about the event for a few moments, then retired to our respective bedrooms with my promise that if I saw it again, I'd call her.

Within a half hour "it" was outside the window again. This time it was different. Hard to describe, but the best to say is that it looked less solid, leaning towards semi-transparent, yet the same basic shape.

I yelled. "Ellen!" I sprang from the sofa towards the window. But by the time I got there it had vanished.

"Where is it?" Ellen asked as she marched to the windows and pulled back her medium-length blonde hair to get a good look.

"Uh, I'm not sure; it *was* there," I hedged, not sure if she would think me nuts.

"What? You woke me up for nothing?" She poked me in the right arm.

"Actually, I did see it; I swear. As soon as I jumped up, it flew over the top of the roof again. But it looked faded, or less solid this time."

"How can that be?" she asked in tired confusion, not expecting an expert answer.

"I don't know. I guess anything is possible with those guys."

Everyone back to bed.

I didn't sleep at all the rest of the night: tossed, turned, and peeked out the windows as if they were three crystal balls into an alien universe. I peeked with sly, barely cracked eyelids, so that I could see well to the windows, but if the probe appeared it would think my eyes were closed.

The invasion started sometime between 4:30 and 5 a.m. It was breathtaking, unimaginable and a total surprise. It wasn't the spinner-probe that I had expected. It was something new. It was unbelievable.

Outside the lower pane of the far right window was a round, flat, filigree object, shorter in diameter by a couple of inches than the actual width of the glass, so that the object was framed nicely by the wood. The alien concoction seemed wafer thin. It resembled one of grandma's old doilies that she put under her living room table lamps. But this one had a streamlined look. My eyes squinted hard for a clear view. I couldn't tell if it was metal, though it was very light gray in color, or if it was made of light, though it was not luminous, nor did it illuminate. The high-tech granny that designed this doily must have used a sheet of laser light and pressed it out of a diamond mold.

It was very close to the glass and moving slowly toward it covering about an inch per second.

Whatever it was, it finally reached the glass window — and kept coming. Slowly, simply, and easily, it passed through the glass storm window, then the inside window, and into my room. This was done without breaking, or scratching, and without sound. It was a technological miracle.

Now, I'd seen alien globes float in the desert near California City, California with my oldest son and his wife; studied the same type globes, plus a saucer, for an hour and a half in the New Mexico desert near Roswell with my friend, Lorraine; and gazed upon more globes in Gettysburg, Pennsylvania with Ellen. These were fun and exciting happenings, maybe even a little daring.

But… "They" were "out there." I was safe when I got home and swooned over my hot chocolate with buttered toast and clicked on the Travel Channel. There were no aliens at home. So when something unexplainable from another world passes unchallenged through your locked bedroom window — when you would normally be asleep and have no knowledge or control of it — this gives one a glacial pause.

The bedroom bore witness to a space invader. Why didn't I take the offensive? Why not jump up and scream, toss a book at it, or throw a plastic bag over it and bolt to the police to collect a reward?

No. A scream may or may not have had any effect. While the spinning globe seemed skittish, the alien-doily had a calm, surrealistic quality about it. Since it passed through glass, maybe a bag, or a book, would pass through it. That would leave me with a damaged book and dented wall. Also, I've never heard of a plastic bag capturing anything bigger than a bee.

Then there is the real reason for no attack from my side. I wanted it there. I wanted to see what happened when this floating piece of magic invaded my space. What wonders might occur? Would I be better off for the experience? Although its presence was a physical invasion, it did not feel invasive. There was no fear, but I remained on red alert.

The alien-doily had passed through glass like a ghost. It halted about one or two inches inside my room. From the upper half of this doily there suddenly launched a slow moving, crystal-clear bubble, about two to three inches in diameter. It resembled a large soap bubble blown by a child from a plastic toy, except that there was no rainbow reflection of light. And like a soap bubble, the alien bubble had zero-thickness. Since the doily was so thin there was no obvious compartment for the bubble to have exited. Its presence stemmed more from a wish, or a finger snap from a Merlin on another world. It made no physical sense that it came from the doily, yet I watched it happen.

As the alien-doily hovered near the window, this crystal bubble flew slowly into my room moving in a straight line at about three inches per second. Of course, there were no lights on in my room, so that the farther the bubble moved into it, darker was the space. The alien doily, after it launched the bubble, slid to the right into the plaster wall and disappeared. Perhaps it went into the back bedroom, which was unoccupied, and I'm sure,

eventually it returned to never-never land. The bubble continued into the dark room, and at about the half-way point it was no longer visible. Its crystal clarity blended flawlessly with its surroundings. Invisible to all from any angle, it was the perfect camouflage.

That's when I sat up.

I looked along the trajectory that the bubble might have followed, but saw nothing. It was gone. Since it could pass through solid objects, perhaps it seeped through my closed bedroom door and out into the hall. Perhaps it hadn't gone anywhere and hung suspended in darkness right in front of me. I'll never know. A slight temptation was to walk to where it was, or might be, and feel around — maybe touch it. Then again, would it burn? Poison me with radioactivity? Paralyze? Maybe I'd leave it alone. I chickened out and returned my head to the pillow.

About a half hour later, the gray spinning probe returned, but vanished the moment I spied it. The First Battle of the Bedroom was over. And, damn, they'd stormed my keep unopposed. I didn't sleep the next two nights, either, though nothing happened.

Colds are something I rarely get anymore unless I'm stressed. However, by the end of that week I had a powerful sinus infection. I was really stressed. These things entering my room at will had me wary. Yet it was wild beyond dreams.

A normal week went by. I worked my customer service job at QVC in West Chester, Pennsylvania. I hiked in French Creek State Park. Ellen and I hung out on the dance floor. The invasion was fading into history.

Then, on a night that felt ominous from the moment of sundown, the final assault began. Sometime after midnight on a cold evening in the middle of the following week, I once again went from deep sleep to instant preparedness. Since the whole feeling was reminiscent of the previous week's episode, I knew instinctively to use my eyes in the slit formation and make as little movement as possible. The alien tactics were almost identical to the previous incident. My squint at the window found the spinning probe watching me. Calling out for Ellen was my first desire, but I withheld.

I'll watch and see what it does, I thought as the device moved slightly back and forth and up and down in an irregular pattern outside the window on the right, never able to stay still, just like before. A moment later it left. And there appeared outside the lower right window a crystal clear globe about the diameter of a man's

head—my head, for instance. This globe, like the bubble, had no measurable thickness. Its surface was perforated with dozens of holes spread uniformly around the object. It moved slowly towards the window pane, and then, like the alien-doily, it glided through solid glass and into my room.

I was excited now. *Wahoo,* here come the aliens again. I was unscathed last time, should be no problem this time. This piece of crystal could be my new best friend.

The holey probe continued slowly into the room. I laid on the sofa on my right side, faced into the room. My eyes felt like electric beams following the ball's far-out process; slit eyelids fooling it all the way. Onward with its aerial march, it traversed the room and reached the back wall just in front of the entrance door. Though it was in dark territory, it was still visible, unlike the bubble, I guess because of its larger, head-size diameter. I took shallow breaths.

Now I'll get a good look at it passing through the door, I thought, figuring I know all about aliens. Just inches from the door, it made a sharp ninety-degree turn to its right, which put it moving directly above my head along the arm of the sofa.

Uh, oh. Here it comes. Now what should I do? The thought had barely cleared the brain's message center when the holey probe was within an inch of the top of my balding head. I had never been so close to an alien object and didn't know what to make of being so now. The probe was near my cranium. Yet I was not afraid. I was fascinated and minuteman ready. All five senses had firing pins cocked, primed to blast a warning if the slightest thing went awry. All these various body conditions and feelings were controlled by me. Nothing else was deciding what I did or felt. No body snatchers were responsible for my actions. I was running my show. What did the probe want?

Then I found out.

Just like it had pressed through the glass, the holey probe pressed about three-quarters of itself into my head. In a moment there was panic, wonder, and then surrender. There was no pain, no discomfort. A sensation was felt, not as strong as a tingle, but definitely perceivable. All my life I had dreamed about contact with extraterrestrials. I wanted it to happen and I wanted it to be good. All the input I'd gotten — "B" movies, sci-fi and science books, the USS *Enterprise* NCC-1701 — everything in life had prepared me. This was it.

But I never foresaw this method. I waited, waited…. Nothing. There were no messages from a distant galaxy that I needed to save the world. No visions of Earth's future after a military holocaust. No talks with God. No enlightenment.

After about fifteen seconds of sub-tingling, the probe disengaged from me. It returned the way it had come, taking its time, floating at the same speed that brought it to me. When it reached the bedroom door it turned right, however, and passed through the solid wood door like a specter, and was gone.

I touched the top of my head to see if I'd been mutilated like the cattle, or if I'd been blessed with a renewed head of hair. Neither. Inventory continued. I got up, and moved around. Everything worked. My head was as clear as ever. There were no side effects. Attitudes about everything were the same as the pre-probe time. I could still think, talk, read, and write. Mental capacity was (sadly) no better, (gratefully) no worse. Nothing had changed for me.

Were there any changes for the foreign species who monitored all this? Since they didn't take anything, maybe they copied all my thoughts, memories, and emotions and were playing them in a loop on their comedy network.

Wait. Something did change. My UFO experience level just vaulted over the Comcast building in Philadelphia. Though I make no pretense that meeting a holey probe compares to the singularity of a close encounter with a living alien, the fact is—one of their civilizations and I touched. How easily it all happened.

Except for my keen awareness to danger (which I attribute to studies in altered-states and meditation) this visit by the holey probe to my body could have been an unknown event. What if in the past my sensitivity had been squashed by too much drink, late hours, or exhaustion? Had I been asleep for any previous visits? For anyone with a little less awareness, with an average sleeping pattern, these near-invisible probes could, and probably do, penetrate sacred places and pop into heads night after night, for years, or for lifetimes, in people all around the world.

Clearly, I am not unique. My experience cannot be the exception. To make such beautiful, effective probes must cost the aliens something. Their information gathering would only pay back if they tapped thousands, maybe millions, of specimens to study the widest comparisons.

And no one would ever know.

Quiet, nearly invisible, remote-controlled—sounds like a 1950s space mag, but it's not.

The invasion is here.

Coatesville, Pennsylvania. Bedroom triple-window that alien devices approached and entered. Entry was through first window on the left, lower pane.

Interior of triple-window. The spinning probe hovered outside. The other probes passed through the closed glass window on lower right and flew across the room. Glass not damaged in any way. This was done in complete silence. Artist's rendering of alien-doily and bubble.

A wider view of the same bedroom. Clothes rack was not there at time of event.

Bedroom door is on right, closet on left. The "bubble" flew through the wood structure of the bedroom door like magic. No damage was done to the door, no residual effects.

Sofa on right is where Medvec observed events. "Holey probe" approached bedroom door, turned right, floated under computer table, and entered top of his head.

Conclusion

Gerard J. Medvec

I am a firm believer in the people. If given the truth, they can be depended upon to meet any national crisis. The great point is to bring them the real facts.

~*Abraham Lincoln*
16th President

My conclusion now is the same as it was at the beginning; that is, it is all real. I hope that some of the stories have illuminated that fact. Perhaps you have learned to make awareness a priority by searching the skies more often, scanning for alien globes while driving through a dark forest, or by taking a second look at that light moving around more than the others near a suburban building. Writing this book has cemented in my own heart and soul how important it all is.

My personal experiences, naturally, have had the most impact on me. The adventures in French Creek State Park culminating with the "Expedition, December 2011," prove that if you seek, you will find. All these occurrences have affected my life in an uplifting way. The knowledge gleaned from my UFO encounters influence how I portray myself to others—sometimes for the good, sometimes as perceived zaniness, I'm afraid. Either way, these events are a big part of who I am. They will never be forgotten and could never be "let go." I would not want to. Therefore, I encourage everyone to visit UFO "hotspots" as reported in *UFOs Above Pennsylvania* and other media to see things for yourself, to *know* rather than just believe.

Another thing I feel compelled to mention: the government denial and disinformation program. I love my country as much as anyone. But it's not perfect. One fall-down spot has certainly been with UFOs. To assume superiority over its citizens by stating that those citizens could not handle the truth about UFOs is a demagogue's attitude and unfit for American leadership. However, I know power and control will make people and governments do strange things.

And there is certainly enough power being wielded by out-worlders to entice even the most humble, free-thinking political leader into covetousness.

When people see something that is unexpected, possibly other-worldly and therefore profound, they instinctively know that it is important, above the norm. Almost everybody has seen almost everything on this planet many times over thanks to the marvels of TV, cable, satellite, fiber optics, movies, Internet, and cell phones. Information flies around our world in seconds. So people know the difference between something distinctly human, and something that is not.

It surprises me, therefore, that when a sighting is reported, the "experts" say that it's most likely:

1. A weather balloon. (Still trying to push that story; are they kidding?)
2. The craft was a military top-secret machine out for a test run.

While the second one does sound like a more plausible expla-nation, it thrusts our otherwise co-vert-loving, let's-create-a-cover-story government, into the realm of The Three Stooges. Why spend billions on a secret flying machine, then send it out over Pittsburg, or even Lycoming County, to have hundreds or more people see it? It makes no sense. In fact, the government would not do it.

The other issue is protection. No government on earth can protect its citizens from alien visitation. Accepted. Tell us the truth and we'll take our chances—and still pay taxes.

Experts have stated that a government's admission that there are things flying over its boundaries that it can't control would lead to that government's collapse. But countries like Mexico, France, Turkey, Italy, and other nations have admitted that they cannot explain every UFO in their skies. This is tantamount to admission of ET visitation. Yet, none of these governments have fallen; none of the religions have dissolved within their borders. All is still as it was. So, to the rest of the governments of the world, why not just admit it. There are beings from other planets visiting Earth! Call it tourism.

Appendix A

The following classification system, developed by Dr. Jacques F. Vallee, may be useful. While the stories in this book are not characterized by sighting type, the system may help those who have had UFO events in their lives and would like a better handle on them:

Classification of UFO Sightings

The Vallee Classification System categorizes UFO sightings using five principal ratings: AN; MA; FB; CE; and SVP, which are divided into three subcategories, labeled SRR, SVR, and PER.

AN Rating
Classifies any anomalous phenomenon

AN1
Anomalies that leave no lasting physical effects, such as lights in the sky and similar phenomena.

AN2
Anomalies that leave lasting physical effects, such as crop circles, scorched earth, and debris.

AN3
Anomalies with associated occupants or entities.

AN4
Interaction of the witness with occupants or entities.

AN5
Anomalous reports of injury or death, such as unexplained wounds, healing of wounds, or spontaneous human combustion.

MA Rating
Describes the behavior of a UFO

MA1
A visual sighting of a UFO that travels in a discontinuous trajectory, such as loops, quick turns, or vast changes in altitude.

MA2
A visual sighting of a UFO with physical evidence, such as burn marks or material fragments.

MA3
A visual sighting of a UFO with living entities on or around the UFO.

MA4
UFO activity, such as maneuvers, accompanied by a change in the observer's perception of reality.

MA5
UFO activity that results in the injury or death of the witness.

FB Rating
Fly-by rating

FB1
A fly-by of a UFO traveling in a straight line across the sky.

FB2
A fly-by of a UFO traveling in a straight line, leaving some kind of physical evidence.

FB3
A fly-by of a UFO traveling in a straight line across the sky, where entities are observed on board.

FB4
A fly-by where the witness experiences a sensation of unreality, i.e., a phantasmagoric state.

FB5
A fly-by that causes permanent injury to, or the death of, the witness.

CE Rating
Close encounter rating

CE1
A visual sighting of a UFO within 500 feet.

CE2
A visual sighting of a UFO within 500 feet with physical evidence.

CE3
A visual sighting of a UFO with entities aboard.

CE4
Abduction of a witness.

CE5
Abducted witness suffers from physical or psychological injuries, or death.

SVP
A Three-digit Credibility Rating

Marks ranging from zero to four are given in each of three subcategories:

1. Source reliability (first digit)
2. Site visit (second digit)
3. Possible explanations (third digit).

SRR
Source Reliability Rating

0 – Unknown or unreliable source.
1 – Report attributed to a known source of unknown reliability.
2 – Reliable source, second-hand.
3 – Reliable source, first-hand.
4 – First-hand, personal interview with the witness by a source of proven credibility.

SVR
Site Visit Rating

0 – No site visit, or answer unknown.
1 – Site visit by a casual person not familiar with the phenomenon.
2 – Site visited by persons familiar with the phenomenon.
3 – Site visit by reliable investigator with some experience.
4 – Site visit by a skilled analyst.

PER
Possible Explanations Rating

0 – Data consistent with one or more natural causes.
1 – Natural explanation requires only slight modification of the data.
2 – Natural explanation requires major alteration of one parameter.
3 – Natural explanation requires major alteration of several parameters.
4 – No natural explanation possible, given the evidence.

Appendix B

AIRPLANE LIGHTS EXPLAINED

Mark Sarro

So many times we look up into the night and see lights flashing across the sky and most of the time we dismiss them as lights on a plane. As I have learned the importance keeping an eye on the sky, I immediately asked myself: "What are the lights on a plane and what do they mean?" So, here are the different lights found on an airplane and what purpose they serve.

Navigation lights:

The aircraft is equipped with a steady light at each wingtip; from the perspective of the pilot the light on the right wingtip is green and the one on the left is red. The purpose of these lights is so that from an outside perspective (i.e., a pilot of another aircraft) can determine the direction that the plane is flying based upon the orientation of these red and green lights.

Position lights:

These are typically steady white lights that are on the edge of each wingtip. They are sometimes on the edge of the horizontal tail, the aft end of the fuselage or at the top of the vertical tail. The purpose of these lights is to improve the visibility of the plane from behind the aircraft.

Anti-Collision Beacon lights:

Two lights are located at the center of the fuselage on the top and bottom of the plane. The lights are reddish orange and rotate to produce a flashing effect. The lights turn on when the first engine is started and remain on until the engines shut down. These lights serve as a warning light to the ground crew to let them know that the engines are on.

Strobe lights:

These are high intensity white lights that are located on each wingtip. Typically, on smaller planes, there is only one light near the leading edge behind the red or green navigation light. The purpose is to draw attention to the plane during flight.

Logo lights:

These are not required by the FAA but are common on larger commercial airliners. They are white lights located on the surface or tips of the horizontal stabilizer.

Wing lights:

These optional lights are white and along the leading edge of the wings. They are used to make the wings more visible during takeoff and landing, as well as for inspecting the wings.

Taxi lights:

This light is a bright white light that is fixed on the landing gear at the nose of the plane. It is used whenever the aircraft is in motion on the ground. It provides better visibility during taxi, takeoff, and landing.

Landing lights:

These are bright white lights that can be found in several locations on the plane, such as the wing root (part of wing closest to the fuselage), the outboard wing (part of wing furthest from the fuselage), or along the forward fuselage. These lights are required during night landings and are useful at airports that are not as well lit.

Runway Turnoff lights:

These bright white lights are along the leading edge of the wing root. They provide side and forward lighting during taxi and when turning off of the runway.

Wheel Well lights:

These are optional lights that can be located in the nose and main gear wheel wells. These lights provide lighting for the ground crew during pre-flight inspections of the plane at night time.

Resources

Filer's Files.com —all short reports
http://en.wikipedia.org —map of Pennsylvania; aviation lights
The International UFO Museum and Research Center, Roswell, NM – all
    short reports
The National UFO Reporting Center (www.ufocenter.com) —all short
    reports
Vallee, Jacques. *Confrontations: A Scientist's Search for Alien Contact.* New
    York: Ballantine Books, 1990
www.aerospaceweb.org —aviation lights
www.brainyquote.com/quotes/authors
www.brighthub.com/science —aviation lights
www.cityofwilliamsport.org/Home/History/tabid/153/Default.aspx
—History of Willamsport, PA
www.fs.usda.gov/wps/portal/fsinternet/!ut/p/c5/04_
—U.S. Department of Agriculture Forest Service
—Allegheny National Forest
www.georgefiler.com —various reports
www.harrisontwp.com/ —History of Harrison Township, Allegheny
    County, Pennsylvania
www.gettysburg.stonesentinels.com/Tours/MainTourMenu.php
—Gettysburg National Battlefield
www.stangordon.info